A GIFT OF
Love

LINDA DELLA DONNA

A GIFT OF *Love*

A Widow's Memoir

ARCHWAY PUBLISHING

Copyright © 2014 Linda Della Donna.

All rights reserved. No part of this book may be used or reproduced by any means, graphic, electronic, or mechanical, including photocopying, recording, taping or by any information storage retrieval system without the written permission of the publisher except in the case of brief quotations embodied in critical articles and reviews.

Archway Publishing books may be ordered through booksellers or by contacting:

Archway Publishing
1663 Liberty Drive
Bloomington, IN 47403
www.archwaypublishing.com
1-(888)-242-5904

Because of the dynamic nature of the Internet, any web addresses or links contained in this book may have changed since publication and may no longer be valid. The views expressed in this work are solely those of the author and do not necessarily reflect the views of the publisher, and the publisher hereby disclaims any responsibility for them.

Any people depicted in stock imagery provided by Thinkstock are models, and such images are being used for illustrative purposes only. Certain stock imagery © Thinkstock.

ISBN: 978-1-4808-0400-5 (sc)
ISBN: 978-1-4808-0520-0 (hc)
ISBN: 978-1-4808-0401-2 (e)

Library of Congress Control Number: 2013922523

Printed in the United States of America

Archway Publishing rev. date: 2/5/14

ELS

Preface

On May 1, 2004, I sat in my kitchen and gazed out a window. In the distance, beyond a flowering plum, over coal-colored rooftops and the hills and dales of a small suburb where I lived in Westchester County, New York, I could see the early morning sun rising brightly in a cloudless sky. The only sounds were those of the breath in my nose, the laughter of two passersby dressed in shorts, the clip-clip-clapping of their sneakers on pavement, and an inner voice whispering over and over, *I promise*. For a long time after the couple had faded from view, I stared blankly at a yellow-eyed grackle strutting about the front yard pecking dirt, and I wondered how I would ever be able to fulfill my promise. It was my sixteenth wedding anniversary, and my husband was dead.

Together to the end; when Edward Louis Sclier breathed his last breath, I was by his side, and my promise whispered in his ear was the last sound he heard.

"I'll write your story," I said. "I promise. I will let the whole world know just what you went through."

I said it. I meant it.

Ed's dying words, *Somebody should*, haunt me.

Through the years, I have tried, without success, to get down on paper the personal story of an ordinary man who loved an ordinary woman in an extraordinary way. I confess I cannot get Ed Sclier's story down on paper. I just cannot do it, and do it justice. I doubt I ever could. This book is more about me. It describes my grief journey, highlights the great man I fell in love with and married, the love we shared, and the woman I have become since my soul mate died. In describing certain events, I am brutally honest, and I know I face a tsunami of criticism for conveying feelings felt at a time when my life turned suddenly upside down. I understand that cancer is a serious illness. Please know that all opinions expressed here in my book regarding cancer and the treatment of it are my own. I know that in some cases, cancer is life-threatening, and I understand there are a lot of treatment options available that have been proven to be successful. Therefore, in no way should my personal opinions contained in this book be taken as advice or direction in any cancer patient's personal treatment decisions. But perhaps, just perhaps, there is one widow out there reading my words, feeling as I felt. If so, and my words reach you, dear *one* reader, then that justifies and validates both of us. For me, it is one goal met and one promise fulfilled. As every widow learns, in order to heal and help fill the void after the death of a spouse, it is necessary and important that she give something back. In addition, in the writing of this book, I intentionally switched from past to present tense in some of the chapters. That said, let the chips fall where they may, and let the universe know, I offer this book up to Edward Louis Sclier in loving postscript: *Accept this book as token of my sincere love and gratitude for all the respect, love, devotion, companionship, support, hope, and confidence you gave me, during and after our marriage. And, please, mark me paid in full.*

My name is Linda Della Donna. This is my story.

Prologue

If you stand on the steps of the Peninsula Hotel in Hong Kong, you can see the sun rise over Central. Across murky water, through a misty harbor haze and pressed into the mountainside, is a sea of skyscrapers the colors of coal, wheat, and cinnamon. Each January, my husband, Edward Louis Sclier, traveled to Hong Kong to attend the annual toy fair held there. Lucky me, as his wife, I got to tag along. For more than seven years, starting each January 1, for several weeks, home was a tony suite at the Royal Garden Hotel in Kowloon. While Ed labored tirelessly in a stuffy hotel room meeting vendors from all over the world, plying his trade of selling giant teddy bears, porcelain dolls, stuffed tigers, multicolored caterpillars, and child-sized rag dolls for Goffa International, I was free to explore cobblestone streets, meet sidewalk vendors, eat noodle soup, shop till I dropped, and bond with my favorite city in the world. One day as I stood on the steps of the Peninsula Hotel gazing into the panoramic view of Central, I swore I heard voices saying someone would die. At the time I was ill and thought the voices meant me.

Later, when I returned to my hotel, I told my husband about the voices and what the voices said. I told him the message frightened me.

He said, "You have some imagination, Linda. You should write a book."

Part I

MY LIFE AS I KNEW IT

- 1 -

GRIEF

*Then finally this big yellow bus came around the corner.
And the brakes screeched very loud. And I had to cover my ears.*

—Barbara Park's storybook character Junie B. Jones

I placed a yellow rose on his chest; kissed his cheek, his forehead, his other cheek. I kissed his nose and lips and said good-night. I hugged him. I love you, I said. Forever, I said. Thank you for being my husband. Thank you for being my best friend.

It is Monday, May 3, 2004. The sky is gray as an elephant's ear, and I am sitting numbly in a funeral parlor mourning the death of my husband. On the long list of ugly, this moment rockets to the top. My son, George, and his girlfriend, Colleen, sit on either side of me. I am surrounded by rows of people dressed in black. All color has vanished from my world. It is as if a light burning brightly simply turned off, and I want desperately to turn it back on, to be someplace else, any place else, and wake up to find this moment a terrible, horrible, giant mistake.

The scent of gladioli, roses, and carnations fills the air. George rises and walks to the center of the room. Extending his right hand, he places it firmly on my husband's casket, bows his head, and pauses. He turns, steps to the podium, and faces the sea of inky mourners. The only sound I hear is the thump-thump of my heart and a thudding hush. My eyes fix on the blanket of roses spread out before me, and through the misty yellow haze the sound of George's voice fades in, fades out, and echoes my brain.

"Ed was my father when my real father was not there for me. I love Ed. He was tough on me. But he did it because he wanted me to be a better man.

"My mother has asked me to say a few words for her. She wants you to know that she is forever indebted to Ed for his love. She says that his love made her feel special for sixteen years. She wishes she could have had sixteen times sixteen years more with the man who accepted her, loved her despite her lumps and bumps, and lovingly helped raise her son, me.

"Ed showed her the magic of travel—Hong Kong, Shanghai, Taipei, Alaska, St. Maarten, Chicago, New Orleans, New Mexico, and more.

"He taught her a sense for business. At least he tried to. She admits she wishes she had been a better student.

"My mother is proud to call herself Mrs. Edward Louis Sclier, and she will cherish his memory and love all the days of her life.

- 2 -

LOVE

*Only people who are capable of loving
strongly can also suffer great sorrow.
But this same necessity of loving serves to
counteract the grief and heals them.*

—Tolstoy

There is a beach in Rye, New York. It sits adjacent to a spinning Ferris wheel on Long Island Sound. One sunny August afternoon amid the raucous laughter of barefoot children at play, I spread my blanket on its sandy shore, unfolded a frayed, multicolored webbed beach chair, and placed it alongside a friend. At the time I was a single parent. When not moonlighting as a waitress, I worked as a secretary for the New York Power Authority. I owned one bathing suit, some pink-and-gray one-piece thing I washed out and hung up to dry each evening after every outing. And thanks to a cheap beach pass, my Macy's marked-down special, and a record high heat wave for the summer of 1986, I spent my weekends at water's edge, gabbing with a strange lady and watching my eleven-year-old son dart about the blistering sand, catching bees in a butterfly net.

"So when are you going to start dating?"

Jill was an untidy woman, someone I'd met at the start of the season. Her skin was wrinkled as a raisin and leathered like an old fisherman's belt. Direct and brutally honest, Jill farted loudly and yelled at babies kicking sand, and at grownups about their kicking-sand kids. She despised flirty girls in bikinis prancing about the shore like pixies in heat and minced no words telling them so; she ordered lifeguards to get the heck down from their tall white towers and go tell muscled, tattooed teenagers at the next blanket to turn down their goddamn radios; she insisted on ogling strange men. In five words, Jill was opinionated, rude, obnoxious, mean, and vulgar. Nobody on the beach liked Jill. Nobody. Except me.

Maybe it was the way Jill handled her meanness, or her candid ability not to give a rat's rear what another person thought about her; maybe it was her Jerry Seinfeld sense of humor always trying to fix me up with some poor stranger, or the way she piled her mop of frizz-balled hair the color of sweet potatoes on top of her sunburnt head; or, maybe it was the kind, loving way she talked to my son when I feigned sleep in my chair because I just didn't have the patience to deal with all those buzzing bees he had collected any more. Maybe it was a combination of all these things. I don't really know. What I do know is that I found Jill to be the funniest person I had ever met. I liked her. She made me laugh—heartily! And whenever I was with Jill, I laughed until I cried.

"Not interested," I said.

"You need to go out on a date. You're too young to be sitting home alone."

In the distance I could see George darting about the beach, his butterfly net swatting air forcefully above his head. A budding entrepreneur, he helped support his salty pretzel habit by offering bee-catching services to nervous sunbathers, charging a nickel a bee, six for a quarter. I waved a high five, the signal to get to the blanket. It was time to eat. I realized if it was the last thing Jill was going to do, she was determined to find me a man. Or die trying. Based on past events, I was afraid she might succeed in finding me a man, as in the time I went for a swim and had asked her to watch my stuff, only to discover upon my return that all my stuff had vanished. In my absence Jill had taken it upon herself to relocate my beach towel, beach blanket, beach chair, beach bag, sunglasses and beach hat, and wouldn't tell me where. After a twenty-minute search combing the beach, I found them. They had been placed neatly on a strange man's chair a hundred yards from where I had left them. The strange man had been taking a swim. I will never forget the look on that man's dripping-wet face, and the embarrassment I felt, as I clumsily scooped up my beach belongings, stuttered an apology, and backed away, smacking butts with another strange man bending over his blanket. Red-faced and tripping, I vowed never to leave Jill alone with my stuff again.

"I'm going to find you a man!" Jill promised. She wagged her finger.

"No, you won't, Jill. No, you won't!"

George laid his butterfly net on the blanket and ran to the water's edge to wash the sand off his hands. When he returned, I handed him a peanut butter-and-jam sandwich, poured him a cup of lemonade, and ordered him to keep an eye on our things while I went to the food stand to buy him a pretzel. I shook my finger at Jill and headed to the far side of the beach. I was busy hopping on alternate feet and didn't notice a man in baggy blue trunks splayed chest down on a king-sized orange bed sheet. He was brown as a berry and had coal-colored eyes, and when I hopped past, he hollered, "Excuse me."

I stopped. I have no idea why.

"My name is Ed Sclier. And I've been admiring you on this beach all summer," he said. "Are you married?"

I didn't answer.

"Are you seeing anyone?"

I changed feet.

"I'll take that as a no. Would you like to have dinner with me?"

And there it was. The *question*. I shook my head.

"Can I have your phone number?"

"I don't think so," I said. And like a scared rabbit, I hopped away.

"Think about it," he yelled. "I know where you're sitting. I'll stop by later and ask again."

Embarrassed, I took the long way back to my blanket, avoiding the strange man.

After George had finished his sandwich and licked the last speck of salt from his pretzel, he picked up his butterfly net, slung it over his shoulder, and dashed off to swat more bees. Unable to contain herself a minute more, Jill broke the silence.

"Who was that man?"

"What man?"

"The man you were talking to."

I'd decided telling Jill the truth outweighed any consequence of telling her a lie. So I confessed that the strange man wanted to take me to dinner and had asked for my telephone number.

"Well, are you going?"

Before I could answer, Jill lowered her reflector, leaned into my face, and glared hard into my eyes.

"Well, you better give him your number or, I promise, I will embarrass you."

I gulped.

It was two hours later. Jill was asleep, or so it seemed, when Ed appeared. Faking a smile as he repeated his request, I quickly scrawled my name and number on a page torn from the Stephen King novel I was reading, the entire time worrying that Jill would awaken and make good on her threat. Handing the crinkled slip to the tanned stranger, all I could think was, *What kind of woman goes out with a guy who uses a king-sized orange bed sheet for a beach blanket?*

Number 37 Washington Place was an aging two-bedroom, white stucco Tudor ranch house set six feet off a busy road. Modest in every way, it mingled with larger, more contemporary two-family dwellings on a winding road off Route 22. Set on the fat side of a pie-shaped corner lot, my house sat directly across the street from a construction company, partially hidden behind a dilapidated weathered stockade fence. Through the broken slats, atop the jagged pointed edges, and in full view of my living room window and entry, like a *Flintstones* cartoon, were a bevy of dump trucks, backhoe loaders, steam shovels, cement mixers, and giant mounds of rock-encrusted earth. Monday through Saturday, 7:00 a.m. to 8:00 p.m., machinery growled and grumbled, digging, dumping, mixing and spinning cement. This was home. It was where I lovingly mowed the lawn, trimmed hedges, raked leaves, tended a garden of tomatoes, string beans, parsley, basil and romaine lettuce, and chose to raise my son, George.

It was a late August night. I was at the kitchen table juggling my checking account, selecting which bills to pay, which bills to leave out, which bills to stick back in a brown paper sack and save for next month to shake up and pick out which bills I'd pay and start the process all over again, when my telephone rang.

"Hi."

It was Ed.

"How are you?"

"Fine. Thank you," I said, sliding the paper sack under a chair cushion.

"I apologize for not calling sooner. I've been away on business. I'm in Chicago. I'll be back in time for this weekend. What are you doing Saturday night? Can I take you to dinner?"

I said I'd have to check my calendar. I didn't have a calendar, but I didn't want Ed to know that. I rustled the brown paper bag I had just hidden, into the receiver, took a deep breath and said, "Hey whaddyaknow, I just happen to be free."

At my feet lay Sammy, my smooth fox terrier. He raised an ear and opened one eye as if to admonish me for my white lie. I pushed his snout away and rustled the brown sack harder.

"Great," Ed said. "I'll pick you up at seven. I'm wearing jeans and a collared shirt. And don't worry. You'll be safe."

I remember thinking as I hung up the phone, *How interesting, how nice, and how thoughtful.* I knew what to wear, and I didn't worry. I felt safe already.

Saturday night arrived with a star-studded sky aglow in full moonlight. Promptly at seven my doorbell rang, and by the light of a golden moon that late summer night, when I opened my door to greet Ed, I got the feeling something good was about to happen. Ed was a radiant vision. Dressed in navy jeans, blue-collared cotton shirt, and polished brown loafers, his eyes sparkled, and his sun-ripened complexion burned bright. I gasped, thinking back to the half-naked man sprawled on an orange bed sheet at the far end of Rye Beach now standing in my doorway fully clothed and looking so damn delicious.

"You clean up nice."

"So do you."

When I stepped out my front door, it was a surprise. It wasn't a surprise. I knew Ed had a good job by the things he had said, and the way he said them. I suspected he made a good living. But what I didn't realize was the effect the kind of car Ed drove would have on me. It was a Cadillac Fleetwood Brougham, and when I saw it for the first time I let out a scream heard above the din and clamor of the roaring cement mixer across the street.

"What's wrong?"

"Your car. Your car," I stuttered.

"What's wrong with my car?"

"It's bigger than my house!"

We drove the Cross Westchester Expressway to I-95. We exited Putnam Avenue and followed it to the top of Main Street. Ed turned left. He parked his Cadillac. The entire time my thoughts were of crazy Jill and my vow to thank her for demanding I go out on this crazy date. Even if it lasted just this one night, I was in heaven. I waited patiently as Ed ran eagerly around the front of the car, swung the passenger door open, swayed to the side, and extended his hand. It was our first touch. He locked my hand to his arm, guided me across the busy street, and held the door while I entered the dimly lit restaurant, The Griffon. Greeted by a maître d', we were guided to a table for two with sidewalk view. The table was draped in crisp white linen. In the center was a squat candle in a fat crystal glass. Ed held my chair, and after I was comfortably seated, he sat opposite me. A waiter appeared and, removing a folded card inscribed *reserved*, asked Ed what we would like to drink. Ed turned in my direction and asked, "Is white wine okay?" I nodded. I smiled. Whatever voice I had was lost in the scream I had made when I left my house. The waiter returned with a carafe of pinot grigio, and after filling our glasses, Ed raised his to mine and looked into my eyes.

"Do you know why I asked you out?"

I had no idea. My heart was pounding hard, and I worried it rustled my knit shirt. I nodded dumbly.

"Well," Ed said, "two reasons—actually three—your (two) legs and your laugh."

I laughed.

Ed smiled, and touching the tip of his wine glass to mine, he said the sweetest words I ever heard.

"You have the most beautiful legs," he said. "And your laugh … well," Ed said, "your laugh can be heard all over Rye Beach. The first time I heard it, I decided anyone who could laugh like that, I had to meet."

We kissed that night. It was our first kiss. It was after we had clinked glassfuls of pinot grigio, toasted a sunny, sandy summer afternoon; exchanged stories about his son's penchant for toy motor cars and my son's fearless bee-catching escapades; dined on filet mignon, coffee, and a slice of cherry cheesecake served with two forks; shared our religions—Ed, Jewish, and me, Catholic—and both agreed that none of that mattered. And after I had laughed—heartily!

- 3 -

GIFTS

*A friend is one who walks in
when the rest of the world walks out.*

—Walter Winchell, from a paperweight Ed gave me

"Do you like Italian?"

We were sitting on Rye Beach, at the water's edge, in matching beach chairs. It was a sunny Saturday, early afternoon. Ed had called me every day for more than a week to say hello. My office morning ritual, sipping a cup of coffee while typing at my desk, now included Ed's daily telephone greeting. Buffalo clouds punctuated a turquoise sky, and I listened attentively as Ed relayed his tale of stopping off on his way home from work earlier in the week to pick out two new beach chairs, one for him, one for me. The orange bed sheet, folded neatly in quarters, lay in the sand behind our new chairs. On it rested a wicker picnic basket filled with food Ed had prepared—tuna with teeny bits of onion mixed with Kraft salad dressing on soft white bread, crusts removed, cut in halves and wrapped neatly in waxed paper; three Claussen half-sour pickles, quartered and rolled in Saran wrap. Oreo cookies and Ritz crackers and chunks of Swiss cheese, each lovingly packed in separate plastic containers—lined the bottom. Taking a bite of half a tuna sandwich Ed passed to me, I asked if he liked ravioli, adding that I make a great sauce. I said it was my mother's secret recipe. I laughed.

"What kind of ravioli?" Ed asked.

"What do you mean?"

"Meat or cheese?"

"Eww," I said, wrinkling my nose. "Why cheese, of course. I hate meat ravioli."

Ed smiled, bit into his sandwich, and winked.

"Do you make meatballs?"

"Best you ever ate," I said. "They're my mother's secret recipe. Would you like to come to dinner?"

I remember Ed smiled, and every time he smiled, I fell more deeply in love with him.

And then Ed said, "Yes."

I raced for time. Ed was due at seven o'clock. I worried I wouldn't be ready. I worried my house was too small, too close to the road, too cluttered, and too old. I moved at Keystone Kops speed, preparing an Italian dinner for my new Jewish boyfriend, the whole time trying not to think about all the shortcomings of my home and the stupid silly sounds emanating from across the street. I was an old-time movie jetting about, mowing the lawn, sweeping the front stone walk, scrubbing floors, and cooking my mother's secret recipes. I had the evening planned to the tiniest detail, bartering new butterfly net with George in exchange for an early bedtime so Ed and I could have private time together. I even gave George the job of making a centerpiece for the dining room table just to get him out of the house so I could clean it and keep it that way.

While George strolled the yard in search of the perfect dandelion and bluest violet, I set the table, polished silver candlesticks, tossed a lettuce salad, dotted it with jumbo-sized black pitted olives, scrubbed the bathroom and cooked. By six o'clock p.m., the table was set, dinner was ready, and George's master centerpiece was placed neatly in the middle of the dining room table. At seven sharp, Ed's hand knuckled the screen door, and, primped perfect, I greeted him.

Every day, strangers cross our paths. From nameless postal carrier delivering mail to faceless lady standing behind a Starbucks counter taking money for morning coffee, life is a daily parade of anonymous individuals entering and exiting our lives. Seemingly, nobody knows who you are, and seemingly, nobody cares, until one day the fickle finger of fate taps you on the shoulder, and you take a chance. In my case, it asked for a telephone number, and I answered the call. Meeting Ed was like catching a falling star; as soon as he walked through my door, sporting his burning smile, looking radiant and tan and holding out a small box, wrapped and ribboned in carnation pink and silver gray, I grabbed tight with both hands and told myself, *Don't ever let him go.*

Ed presented me with a gift that night, and as soon as he placed it in my hands, I ripped every piece of wrapping off that present. I discovered a pink, white, and gray ceramic coffee mug inscribed with a famous Emerson quote: *A friend is a gift you give yourself.* I took that poetic verse as a sacred sign from above, and it was all I needed to move forward in learning more about Ed. Wiping a tear of joy from one eye, I threw my arms around him, pressed my lips to his, and kissed him.

And guess what?

He kissed me back.

My little house had a dining room. Set between the living room and kitchen, it held an oblong dining table with six matching cane-backed chairs. Displayed prominently in a matching china closet were my treasured family heirlooms—four assorted fruit plates (a gift from a high school classmate) bordered in cobalt blue and bearing a different image of banana, apple, orange, or purple grapes centered in a field of snow white. Resting on the top back shelf were six larger plates bordered in harvest gold with a bouquet of wheat tied neatly in a bow the color of caramel and centered in a field of white. These were prized trophies, like Cracker Jack prizes, that my late mother had collected from weekly purchases of boxes of Duz laundry detergent at a local supermarket. There was also a collection of rose-budded English bone china teacups, each with matching saucers, classic finds I had discovered at a garage sale. Included in my gallery of treasures were the favorite Waterford crystal sugar bowl and creamer, items purchased especially on layaway at B. Altman's, back in the day when I worked my first secretarial job, for Nestlé at 100 Bloomingdale Road.

With lights dimmed and candles lit, I placed a large platter brimming with cheese-filled ravioli and a bowl of tossed salad dotted in jumbo-sized black pitted olives on the dining room table. Never mind that a cement mixer chugged noisily across the street and sounds of machinery growled through the open screen door and windows; it was home sweet sweeter sweetest home watching Ed eat the plate of cheese ravioli and side of salad layered in black olives that I had just served him. I made the perfect host, and Ed made the perfect guest. With no encouragement from me, Ed asked for second helpings and complimented George, saying, "Linda, everything is delicious," and "George, did you make that centerpiece? Adding dandelions and violets was a wise choice."

Holding one limp violet between two fingers, Ed said, "Hey, George, did you ever think about making table centerpieces and selling them for profit?"

Rising quickly from my chair and cupping two hands over George's ears, I begged, "Please don't give him any ideas."

Chocolate cake frosted in gooey chocolate icing was dessert. Laughing loudly, I sliced it large and chunky, and licked my fingers. Plopping a piece on Ed's plate, I said, "Every man likes chocolate cake. Don't they?"

After the table was cleared, after dishes were washed, dried, and neatly put away, after George was tucked in bed and his prayers heard, Ed and I retreated to the living room, but not before I cut a second helping of chocolate cake—one for Ed, one for me—and poured two cups of coffee: mine in my new ceramic mug, Ed's in a delicate rose-budded china tea cup. Cuddled together on the living room sofa, facing the TV, Ed gulped forkfuls of cake while I made plans for our upcoming weekend. Ed and I were falling in love, and what better place to make our love grow than a return visit to Rye Beach, sitting at water's edge, in matching beach chairs, sharing secrets, eating leftover doughy cheese ravioli in a fat round thermos, salad dotted in jumbo-sized black pitted olives in plastic containers, and chocolate cake oozing melted chocolate icing on wax-coated paper plates, alongside a king-sized orange bed sheet and laughing—heartily.

It was after Ed and I had moved to Rye Brook some two years later that I learned of Ed's deep dislike for cheese, chocolate, and olives. As a surprise, I invited his good friend, and his good friend's girlfriend, to our new home for dinner. I wondered what would be appropriate to serve a nice Jewish couple. If you guessed cheese ravioli, salad dotted in jumbo-sized black pitted olives, and chocolate cake iced in gooey chocolate for dessert, you guessed right.

Ed was a gracious host, boasting to his good friends how happy he was to be married to his beautiful Italian wife, Linda. He bragged, "My lovely wife, Linda, can cook, and," he said, with broad smile, "Linda's not just a good cook, she's a great cook." I blushed, believing every word, the whole time filling plates with doughy cheese-filled squares, salad greens peppered in jumbo-sized black pitted olives, and chunks of chocolate cake iced in chocolate. At the end of the evening, Ed's friend, his lips iced dark chocolate, said I did a good job stealing Ed's heart. Feeling his bear-hug arms around me and saying good-night, I beamed with pride, until the jovial guy added what a shock it was to see Ed eat cheese and chocolate and black olives. He said, "Never mind the cheese in the ravioli and the olives in the salad. I can't believe Ed eats chocolate cake!" Then he planted a kiss on my cheek and howled, "Congratulations!"

It was after our guests had left and Ed and I were alone that I said something. I was at the sink feeling silly, stupid, and dumb, the entire time scraping leftovers into the garbage disposal, rinsing dishes, and asking in a growly voice, "Why didn't you tell me you didn't like cheese ravioli? Or olives? Or chocolate cake?"

In an instant Ed appeared at my side. He sank his two hands into the sink filled with soapy hot water and grabbed mine. Smiling, he shook his head and said softly, "I didn't want to hurt your feelings."

I let out a breath, and through teary eyes I said, "Let's clear this mess and get to bed."

After that night, cheese, olives, chocolate, or food the color black was never served in our house again. My man preferred ravioli stuffed with meat, salad sans black olives, and angel food cake pure as driven snow.

And that was that.

There is a tall building the color of silver in White Plains, New York. It sits on a busy corner of a tree-lined street opposite the Galleria Mall. In the rising sun, its sealed windows glisten like glass particles in wet sand. It is Monday, April 6, 1987, and the air is clear, the sky is blue, and except for puddles of melting snow drooling along sidewalks and busy streets, the earth is dry. I park my 1979 Datsun 210 in the underground garage, ride the elevator to the twelfth floor, and rush to my desk. It is another start of another week in my busy life as secretary at the New York Power Authority, where I work for two project managers and support an engineering staff of eighteen men and women. It is the days before high-speed internet, computer screens, and racing keyboards. To keep up with daily deadlines and mounting secretarial requests, I must rely on an electric IBM Correcting Selectric typewriter with bouncing metal ball to get a job done. I sit at a desk located down the hall from Mr. LeRoy Sinclair, president and chief operating officer, and sandwiched between two project managers. Mr.

Sinclair is the nicest executive I have ever met. Each morning he makes his way from elevator to office at end of hall, stops at my desk, greets me by my first name, and asks how George is, and waits for my answer. I have tremendous respect for this man and the polite, professional, friendly way he treats me, and all employees regardless of rank.

My work space is an alcove. Think three-sided jut in the wall off a crowded hall and one giant-sized floor-to-ceiling window with picture-perfect view of middle Westchester and distant county airport. At NYPA, an alcove work space is considered prime real estate, and I am the envy of all coworkers. An alcove is designed specifically for executive secretaries and middle management. I am neither. The common belief is that NYPA simply ran out of space and I got lucky. *Or maybe not.*

One of my managers, Mr. J (not his real initial), is a scrawny man with unmanageable hair. He wears tailored suits with knife-creased pants and speaks in squeaky short sentences. He is impatient, demanding, and nosy, and micromanages the people under him. Nobody wants to be his secretary. On the long list of difficult bosses, it is no secret that I drew the short straw. The reason I put up with Mr. J, as I tell my friends when they ask me why I put up with this lunatic, is that my son has this nasty little habit—he likes to eat. Then I get back to work. I figure the alcove is just reward for pain and punishment endured, and the true reason I got the coveted office space with Kodachrome view. An act of God? Just reward? I leave it to you, dear reader, to decide. But I like and appreciate that no one can see me pound a keyboard while I get my work done and put up with the grief. Thanks to that private, secluded space, I sparkle like a lit firecracker in a dark place while learning the importance of a healthy work environment.

It is eight o'clock a.m., and my fingers are dancing across the keyboard at lightning speed. Earlier, Mr. J presented me with a typing job, an agenda, and a thirty-page specification outlining the proposed condensate polisher facility to be built at NYPA's Indian Point nuclear power plant located in Buchanan. He needs this work for a meeting with his boss, vice president Admiral Early. The meeting started ten minutes ago. Mr. J says he did not see the meeting penciled in on his calendar posted on the wall by the door in his office until just now, and he says he does not recall seeing my handwritten reminder scrawled on bubble-gum-pink paper and Scotch-taped to his chair yesterday morning. He says he has no idea where the memo is, the one I handed him two weeks ago highlighting the date, time, and place of this meeting, and he swears he never saw it and that I never gave it to him. He says, hurry up, Linda. He says, I need the item in your typewriter, Linda. He says, I need it now, Linda. I smile. He goes away. I type. It is seconds later, and Mr. J pops out of his office and peeks around the wall. He takes two steps and stands over me. He does this in between buzzing me on the intercom and asking, is it ready? Yet? When? And then he says, I need it now, Linda. Where is it, Linda? Can you please, Linda? He does this several times more, and I do not answer. I smile. I type. When I speak, it is to assure Mr. J he will have his work ASAP, but I say, you will need to let me just type. I say these words sweet sweeter sweetest. But inside I grumble. It is the beginning of a long, hard day.

This particular morning the telephone on my desk rings. It is my personal line. I figure it is Ed calling to say hello and wish me good morning. At the same time the light on my intercom flashes. It is Mr. J and I know he is buzzing to remind me he needs his agenda and specification. I press the ringing telephone button, thinking I will hear the sound of Ed's voice. I think I will tell Ed to please hang on. I hold the receiver to my ear and open my mouth to speak, and just then, out the corner of one eye, I spy Mr. Sinclair rounding a corner at the far end of the hall. Anticipating his arrival at my desk at any moment, I sit at attention, hesitating to speak into the telephone, when the voice on the other end blurts a good morning. It is Ed. Without taking a breath, and before I can interject a word, he says, Linda, it's a beautiful day, spring is sprung, good time to sell a house. Call your broker. Time for us to find a place to live. There is a click in my ear, and the dial tone sounds, a signal Ed hung up. The intercom punctuates the air and interrupts my thought process. I look up and see Mr. Sinclair, briefcase in one hand, folded newspaper in the other, standing over my desk.

Good morning, Linda. How are you, Linda, and how is George? He smiles and waits for my usual pleasant response.

I have no idea how much time has elapsed, but I sit there, dumb as a stump, telephone in one hand, intercom button flickering and buzzing, my mouth open and no words coming out of it. Mr. Sinclair repeats, good morning, Linda, how is George? And the intercom grows silent. It buzzes. Again. Again. And again. I am wide-eyed and staring into space, the only thought in my brain Ed and Ed's words. ... *Put your house on the market. Time for us to find a place to live.*

I am steeped in mental fog, as Mr. Sinclair and, now, Mr. J stand over me asking if I am all right. There is a long silence, and I nod numbly. Laying the phone on my desk, I whisper to both men that I am fine, but my weak voice is not convincing, and they do not believe me. They are certain I have just received bad news; perhaps the news is about my son, George. A new discussion begins, and it is as if I am invisible. They talk about me in the third person. Mr. Sinclair says to Mr. J, she should leave work. He says, it is okay if she must. Mr. J nods to Mr. Sinclair in agreement, but the look on his face says, *Not until she gets my specification and agenda typed.* Only he does not say that to Mr. LeRoy Sinclair, president and chief operating officer of the New York Power Authority. It takes time for me to convince both men that I am okay, especially Mr. Sinclair. I say that if I must leave the office for an emergency, I will not hesitate. Mr. Sinclair smiles, nods, and trails off to his office, telling Mr. J without turning his head that he should take better care of me. Mr. J, red-faced, nods and disappears into his office, shutting the door behind him, his precious meeting and document in my typewriter no longer a topic of concern.

Dumbly, I swivel my chair and gaze out my window into the endless sky and distant view, spying a rising airplane with a tail of smoke the color of snow tracing its speeding path. I pick up the telephone and dial Ed. At the sound of his voice, I say hello. I say I have one question. I say, "Did you just ask me to marry you?" The airplane courses closer, soars higher. Ed is quiet and the silence is deafening. I am concerned I just embarrassed myself. My eyes fix on the airplane skywriting the teal sky, and my thoughts ramble and race. *We are a couple. We are not a couple. It is months we are dating. I am not sure. I am sure. I know he has feelings for me. I know I have feelings for him. Damn! Why is there silence?* I inhale. The plane soars higher nearer closer and centers my windowed view. I worry that any moment Mr. J will pop his head out of his office, peek around the wall, tower over my desk, and demand his agenda and thirty-page specification, and I will have to hang up on Ed before he answers. I worry Mr. LeRoy Sinclair will return to check on me and ask, is everything okay, Linda? Do you need to leave the office, Linda? And the same silly scenario I experienced a moment before will instant replay. The mounting airplane continues its scribble in the endless sky when finally a voice breaks the silence. I blink, because out my window I can almost see spelled out in smoke-puffed perfect letters, the word *y-e-s* just whispered in my ear. I am unable to speak. No words come out of my mouth. Again. The only sound is the rhythmic music of Ed's laughter flooding my brain.

I hang up the telephone, swivel my chair face forward, my back to the window, to see Mr. J glaring down at me. Sufficiently recovered from his encounter with our president, he stares at the blank sheet of paper in my typewriter and says, where is my agenda, Linda? He says, do you have it, Linda? He says, where is my specification, Linda? He says, I am sorry to disturb you, Linda, but I must have them. I must have them now. I smile. I type. With or without my precious alcove, this is my magic moment, and nothing Mr. J says or does bothers me. Not today, tomorrow, or the rest of my days at NYPA.

- 4 -

FRIENDSHIP

The biggest thing is to be grateful for every moment.

—Michael Gates

Ed and I had been traveling around with a broker, house hunting for days. Dressed in oversized shirt, leggings, and chubby socks, and sporting a sparkly diamond on my third finger, left hand, I smiled prettily as we walked the rooms of each prospective home the stately woman from Century 21 showed us, while Ed waited patiently for a smile, blink, or any positive sign from me that perhaps the one we were walking through was the one I liked. It didn't happen. Nothing pleased me. Bedrooms were too small or situated too close to the master bedroom; closets were tiny or nonexistent; bathrooms were horrid; one in particular stands out in my mind: a putrid chipped pink tile combined with slate gray fixtures, and a tub with an indelible rust ring. In every instance the kitchen needed updating. For three more days we continued our search for a place where Ed; his son, Matthew; his cat, Samantha; George; my dog, Sammy; and I could live. By midweek we were exhausted.

One Monday evening, we sat in my living room, sipping coffee and watching Dynasty, reviewing our options. I listened attentively while Ed discussed pluses about each house we had inspected. The house in Mamaroneck, he recalled, had a view of the golf course, the condo in Greenwich required no yard work, and the place in Harrison was walking distance to the duck pond and middle school. My eyelashes began to ache thinking about all the different homes we had seen, the different options available, and all the changes happening way too fast for me. I looked around at my cozy Tudor ranch with its *Flintstones* view and realized I was not 100 percent sold on the idea of making a move. When *Dynasty* broke to commercial, I turned to Ed and said, "It is not a good idea." I said, "I liked that we have separate homes and separate living arrangements." I said, "I do not want to get married and that maybe it isn't such a good idea after all, at least not at this time." I said, "It will be difficult to blend two families." Ed's son was three years older than my son, and I disliked the idea of the boys possibly having to share a bedroom, even if it was only on visits. I worried about being the only female in the household, and I was uncomfortable with that. Seeing what was on the market in our price range, "Well," I said, "I am concerned for everyone's privacy and comfort, mostly mine."

Ed got quiet, very quiet, and when the eleven o'clock news came on, he removed his arm resting around my shoulder, got up, walked to the door, and kissed me good-night. It was a long, passionate kiss. Then he left.

I figured that was it. I figured that was Ed's way of saying goodbye. Maybe we would be a couple but would just live apart.

The following day my telephone rang. I was sitting at my desk, and it was Ed. He said he wanted me to meet him and a realtor in Harrison. "Opposite the duck pond on Harrison Avenue," he said.

He said to be there at two o'clock p.m. He said, "I have a house I want you to see."

The house at 212 Betsy Brown Road was brand-new, with 3,300 square feet and a two-car garage, and sat handsomely on a tree-lined street in an upscale neighborhood in Rye Brook, New York. Boasting an open floor plan with a hammered-copper canopy front bay window that glistened like a new penny in the afternoon sun, this gorgeous contemporary sported four bedrooms, step-down living room, family room with catercorner fireplace, white Poggenpohl cook's kitchen leading to a formal dining room with glass sliders, wrap-around deck, and a master bedroom suite with a walk-in closet big enough to park a Miata. It left me breathless. But, truth be told, it was the vaulted sky-lit entry splashing sunshine that did it for me. Built as the model home for a dozen custom homes on surrounding Candy Lane, this magnificent house personified elegance and seemed to call my name that radiant spring day in 1987 when I first planted one high-heeled toe inside. Standing next to Ed, beneath the majesty of all that white light raining down on us, I let out a great big scream—much to Ed's and the Realtor's surprise. I could not help myself. Whatever deal Ed had planned on making with the builder that bright afternoon would be tough after my open display of emotion. But if Ed was unhappy with me, he did not show it. Instead, he took my hand and walked me room to room, insisting I be absolutely sure about living in this house and wanting to know if there was anything I would change if I had the choice.

When I calmed down, I realized there was. I said, "I don't like red tile on the fireplace." I said, "I'd like gray tile instead." Then, I added, getting carried away with myself, I'd like a wall separating the den from the kitchen. Just like that, Ed made it happen, and he made it part of our deal. The only thought watching this man in action was of one sunny August afternoon on a sandy beach in Rye, meeting a half-naked man sprawled on a king-sized orange bed sheet, calling out to a stranger. Like the *Sun* newspaper's response to the letter from a wide-eyed kid asking the world-famous question if Santa Claus was real, I repeated over and over to myself, *yes, yes, yes*. Looking around at our find, at the man holding my hand, and the diamond wrapped neatly around my finger, I blessed myself one trillion times, times one trillion times more. I was home. I was really home. Home to a place I had never been and wanted never to leave. The instant Ed gave his nod of approval to the broker that this was the house he and I would buy, I threw my arms around him and squeezed hard. Then I pinched my sleeveless arm until it turned red as a plum. Ed's eyes grew large as saucers. He said, "What are you doing?" I said, "I am making sure I'm not dead and that I didn't dream you up, or the house we're standing in."

Ed didn't say much. He wasn't a chatty kind of guy, but I knew by his wet eyes he was choked with emotion. He had succeeded in reeling me in, putting a smile on my face, and demonstrating how much he truly loved me, a lesson that in the course of our union would repeat itself time and again.

It was late August when we closed on 212 Betsy Brown Road. Renovations to my specifications completed and our separate residences sold, separate moving trucks and separate teams of movers arrived at Ed's townhome in Port Chester and my house in North White Plains to load our belongings and move us into our new home. My boxes packed, closets, attic and basement emptied, and all my furniture loaded successfully on a truck, I gathered George and Sammy into my Datsun loaded with linens and followed a moving truck down Route 287 East to Rye Brook. I was on my way to becoming Mrs. Edward Louis Sclier.

Dressed in cutoffs, old tank top, and sneakers, with ponytail and no lipstick, and toting a dank rag doused in water and lemon oil, I wiped everything clean as it came off the moving trucks. Standing in the doorway, dusting furniture and directing sweaty movers where to place each piece, I noticed Ed's knitted brow, a sign that he worried I was working too hard. He kept racing from inside the house to outside the house to ask if I needed to take a break. He wanted to know if I needed a drink of water. He said, "Maybe you need to sit down, Linda." He said "Linda," and was about to ask me something else, when a woman from a big house across the street marched up our driveway. Ed disappeared into the house, leaving me to greet our new neighbor alone. I was sweating, ragged as an old rag doll, and my hair resembled a fright wig, but I smiled like a circus clown at my new, perfectly coifed, dressed-in-silk-slacks-with-matching-cardigan neighbor. A short while later I stepped inside the house, holding my sides and laughing. Ed asked, "What's so funny? Who is that woman? What did she want?" I said that was our new neighbor and that she wanted to know, "do I got Wednesdays free". I laughed again. Ed did not. He said, "That will never happen again," and he dubbed me with my new middle name—Please. "Linda Please," he said, "go sit down. Linda Please, take a rest. Linda Please, do it for me."

Then he smiled. "Linda," he took a breath and put his arm around me. "Please?"

For six years, Ed and I lived the good married life in Rye Brook. I met Ed's friends and family and accompanied him on numerous business trips. I met his boss, secretary, admin assistant and made friends with all of his business associates. When Ed spoke of his son, Matthew, or my son, George, he referred to the boys lovingly as *our* boys or *our* sons, and I was introduced as *My lovely wife, Linda*. Life with Ed was one long date—he raced to open and hold doors for me, and got annoyed if I forgot to let him. When we were out, he held my hand and if we saw a movie in nearby Greenwich, he rested his arm around my shoulders and pulled me close.

I cannot count the number of times or remember the reasons Ed stopped and purchased a bouquet of Sonia roses, my favorite flower, before boarding his train from Manhattan to Port Chester, to present to me, but I can recall with certainty his smile and outstretched arms showing them off each time he walked through the door, saying, "I just wanted to make a surprise."

It seemed Ed was always *making* a surprise especially for me. He returned from business trips with small presents. One in particular looms large in my mind—a sky-blue T-shirt emblazoned with a large Monarch butterfly across the front. When he lifted it out of his suitcase and gave it to me, he said, "Linda, soon as I saw it I thought of you. I have no idea why."

As the years rolled by, I was struck by Ed's strong self-discipline and genuine thoughtfulness. Every morning he rose at five a.m. and got ready for work—in the dark. When I questioned why, he said, "If I turn on the light, I will disturb your sleep."

When Ed finished dressing quietly, he tiptoed out the room, down the carpeted staircase to make breakfast—two slices of buttered toast and a cup of coffee to go. He'd scarf down a daily vitamin, sip a glass of orange juice, admire his garden, feed his cat, walk my dog, and clean the counter. He'd wash his eating utensils, too; then he'd tiptoe back up the stairs, into the bedroom to place a kiss on my sleepy forehead, a polite reminder my alarm was about to go off. Later, after I was up, dressed, out the door, and seated at my desk, my telephone would ring. It was Ed. "Good morning, Linda. Just checking in."

When my nose was too stuffed, if I had a migraine or bad period cramps, when my back was out or I had a fever and was too weary to drag myself out of bed to make the drive to the drugstore to fill a prescription, Ed was there for me, insisting, "Linda Please, let me do this for you."

Summers in Rye Brook were spent outdoors. We gardened—Ed planted tomatoes and string beans, I planted petunias and geraniums. We entertained our boys making ice cream sundaes on a picnic table—the old fashioned way with a homemade ice cream maker—and barbecued. I set the table, and Ed did the grilling.

Cold weather, when Matthew was away at school and George was busy with friends, we worked at decorating our new home. I picked out the wallpaper, and Ed papered the walls sending George and me to a movie, his treat, while he performed the task. Weeknights, after work, we shopped for groceries—together. Ed did the driving and pushed the grocery cart, insisting when we got home he would do the cooking, because I looked tired from working all day, and as he often said, "Because I worry about you, Linda. That's why."

Life was not without sorrow while living in my dream house with my dream mate. Betsy Brown Road was a busy thoroughfare with a double yellow line that ran from a traffic light at the top of our street to the full stop sign at the next corner. A constant worry were speeding cars, roaring motorcycles, and lost rigs making deliveries all aiming to beat the yellow light. The third year we were living in Rye Brook, while Ed was away on a business trip and Matthew was at school, Ed's cat got hit by a car. She was killed. My neighbor, Donna B, heard the thud from her kitchen window and called me at work to relay the sad news.

In no time, I was home to dig a hole for Ed's cat feeling tremendous guilt the entire way. I was the one who let Amanda out of the house before leaving for work that morning. After the hole was dug, George and Donna B at my side, I respectfully laid Amanda to rest. And for the sake of George, I said a prayer. And without thinking, I fashioned two ice cream sticks into the shape of a cross and placed it on the grave.

Two days later, when Ed returned home from Chicago, I broke the news. Ed got quiet. I just kept talking like a fool. I offered my sincerest condolences and apologized over and over again for letting Amanda out of the house, saying, "It was all my fault," and "I'm so sorry. I'm so, so sorry."

Guiding Ed out the sliding doors, the same doors I had let Amanda out of just three days before, I took Ed by the hand and led him into the back yard. I pointed to where I had buried Amanda. Head lowered in shame, I knelt beside the tiny grave and prepared myself for what I expected to be an emotional and perhaps angry response. But as usual, it was Ed who was there to support me. Because when I looked up, what I saw was a man staring down at a mound of dirt freshly dug with homemade stick cross jutting out of it, with a grin splashed across his face.

"What's so funny?"

"My cat was Jewish."

And then it happened. Our boys were grown. And for different reasons they lived away from home, attending different schools in different states, prompting our decision to put 212 Betsy Brown Road on the market. Ed saying, "It's time for us to go find a less expensive place to live."

Ed was from New Haven. He secretly missed small town life and living in a rural area. He enjoyed planting vegetables, the squawking of a yellow-eyed grackle and swooping hawks. He missed the heartbeat of a quiet wooded view. So, when he suggested the state of Connecticut to look for our next home, I agreed, keeping in mind that I liked to write, and secretly yearned for a separate room for a home office, space for a dog and a cat, and extra bedrooms for *our* boys when they came home on visits. With all this in mind, one bright Sunday morning, Ed and I piled into the Cadillac with the dog and headed north. One hour and fifty-something miles later, ambling down Route 7, a winding two-lane country road, we came to a steel bridge. Ed said, "This looks like an interesting bridge," and before I knew it, he hung a right, and we stumbled upon New Milford, a quaint New England village with unspoiled panoramic mountain and lake views.

We decided to investigate this new area and to do it on foot. Ed drove to the blinking traffic light, turned left and parked in the train station lot directly across from Connecticut Memories, an antique store. Sammy in tow, we tumbled out of the car and crossed the cobblestone street, where we stopped to admire a weathered wooden birdcage hanging from a tarnished brass chain in the store's window.

Following a row of potted marigolds and purple petunias down a red-bricked pavement, we walked to the opposite corner, crossed Bank Street, and peeked into the window of a bookstore. On display were eight half-opened children's books. Immediately, I was reminded of a box of Crayola crayons as their neon colors glistened in sunshine. As we worked our way up the street, the aroma of freshly ground coffee and cinnamon wafted through the air. The pleasing odor was from the Coffee Café.

We inched along the street, past the movie theater sign saying *Mrs. Doubtfire,* past a dusty-windowed five-and-dime store and the hot wings take-out place. We crested the hill and discovered Main Street and a tree-lined village green complete with gazebo. As we stood there admiring the Currier and Ives view, a burst of loud laughter suddenly poured from the open windows of a passing Ford station wagon. I turned my head and spied a car seemingly overflowing with noisy, animated children. And I recognized the driver—it was none other than Mia Farrow.

I looked at Ed. He looked at me. He smiled. I smiled. And both of us at same time asked, "What do you think?"

We walked to a nearby Realtor's office. Together we examined the Multiple Listing book, looking at pictures of homes for sale. But, nothing moved me. I glanced at a galley of photos pasted on a front window and one caught my eye. When the woman behind the desk asked Ed if there were something of interest she could show us, he pointed in the direction I was looking and said, "I want to see the one my wife is smiling at."

Next thing I knew, Sammy was waiting in the Cadillac, Ed was holding my hand, and we were walking inside the house in the picture—a darling four-bedroom townhouse—canary-colored, free-standing, with crimson front door and two-car attached garage in the Sullivan Farm condominium complex.

This home had a loft. I thought home office. Ed and I stepped into the backyard, and I could almost hear Ed's thought: *This is where I plant tomatoes.*

We were far from the madding crowd, and far from our jobs. The air was clean and crisp. Clasping Ed's hand, I turned to him and said, "I like it."

And just like that, in typical Ed fashion, he made it happen.

In what seemed like no time, Ed and I were packed and moved into our new home in Sullivan Farm. With no lawns to mow, no sidewalks and driveways to shovel, and no boys to pick up after, we had more time to spend with each other, and our passions. When not working and driving to our respective jobs, we explored our new venue. We went to the movies at the Bank Street Theater, attended outdoor concerts on the village green, and Saturdays and Sundays, we enjoyed coffee with warm cinnamon rolls at the Bank Street Coffee Café. Ed made a garden—planted tomatoes, basil, string beans, and lettuce. I scribbled in cheap spiral notebooks. In summer, we sat in matching beach chairs at water's edge on Candlewood Lake. Winter weekends, we skied Woodbury Mountain. Together, we read, watched television, walked Sammy, played gin rummy or checkers, and thoroughly enjoyed each other's company. Regardless of the state of the economy, what nonsense our boys had done to test our patience, or what was happening in the world of politics, all of it mattered little to Ed and me. We were like two chips in a cookie rolling joyously along.

Once again, sadness paid a visit. This time, my beloved Sammy, the dog Ed jokingly and lovingly referred to as his step-dog, died. And because of all my weeping, Ed insisted I have a new puppy. "Linda Please," he said, "I can't stand it if you're unhappy." Less than two weeks after cremating Sammy, we adopted a new fur baby. Our new puppy looked just like Sammy. We named him Izzy.

Snow fell. Snow melted. Spring became summer, summer became fall and before I knew it, we had lived in Connecticut three years, and my hundred-mile-round-trip daily commute to my office in White Plains proved to be an impossible hardship for me. One afternoon on my way home from work, I fell asleep behind the wheel. My car veered off the road. I snapped awake just in time. When I relayed my frightening experience to Ed, I saw a furrow in his brow. Less than a week later, Ed announced, "We are moving back to Westchester." And the next thing I knew, we had sold another residence, packed our bags, and tagged a moving truck, this time to a two-bedroom townhome in Hartsdale, Ed saying, "Linda Please, give me six more years until I retire; then we'll find a little house with a place for a dog and a cat, someplace I can garden and someplace you can write. We'll travel, see the world, visit *our* boys and we'll do it together. *I promise.*"

With Rye Brook and Connecticut behind us, Hartsdale was home now. We unpacked our bags, arranged the furniture, and settled in. Life was good. But I yearned to write. Full-time. After discussion with Ed, in December 2002, at age fifty-something, I made the decision to take an early retirement package from NYPA and wait for Ed to turn sixty-five years and six months, his target age to retire from his job. I started to work as a freelance writer, took online and correspondence writing courses, and graduated from the Institute of Children's Literature. I submitted my work to editors and publishers and collected clippings and my fair share of rejection letters. I got published in *Westchester Parent magazine,* a local parenting publication, and the *Journal News,* the local newspaper. I joined the Society of Children's Book Writers and Illustrators and attended writing seminars and writing workshops. I began writing articles for children based on my travels to Hong Kong, wrote query letters, worked on submissions, and collected more rejection letters. I didn't care, because I felt blessed that I had Ed and was living my dream.

Ed's sixty-fourth birthday and the anniversary of living in Hartsdale dawned. At the sight of Ed blowing out birthday candles on a homemade white layer birthday cake, I embraced him, saying how lucky and how blessed we are. I exclaimed, "Looks like we'll get to do all those things we planned!"

- 5 -

HEAVEN

Where you used to be, there is a hole in the world, which I find myself constantly walking around in the daytime, and falling in at night. I miss you like hell.

—Edna St. Vincent Millay

It is a cold, windy morning. Tall buildings in mirrored glass reflect a gray sky. A fishing boat has capsized in the East River, and blaring sounds from sirens racing to the harbor reach the shore. I am dressed in an antique white lace dress, and a spray of baby's breath forms a barrette for my hair. I clutch a lily-of-the-valley nosegay dripping in white satin ribbons in my left hand and clasp Ed's hand with my right, as we lead a procession of well-wishers: Matthew; George; my dad, Frank; my brother, Richard; his friend Jody; Ed's sister, Judy; and her husband, Dr. Jim. We walk through a misty morning rain from a parking garage on First Avenue to 77 United Nations Plaza. It is May 1, 1988, Ed's and my wedding day.

Behind closed doors and in the privacy of a candlelit chapel, far removed from the sound of screaming ambulances, fire engines, and police cars racing madly to the nearby harbor accident, an organist plays and a soprano soloist sings *You Light Up My Life*. Dad clasps my arm and guides me gently down a golden oak aisle to Ed, the man I have consented to marry. Ed stands before me, poised on crimson carpeted steps, hands folded neatly at his waist. He is dressed in a blue three-piece business suit with threads of pink running through it, and his collared shirt, blue as the summer sky we met under, is buttoned in pearl white. Our eyes meet. Dad leans into my face, tightens his arms around my waist, and plants a kiss on my forehead. Clasping Ed's hand to mine, he gives Ed a nod of approval and steps to the side.

Because we do not wish to offend anyone, Ed and I have elected to be married by a Unitarian minister in a nondenominational chapel. We write our vows and request that the words "until death do us part" be stricken from the ceremony.

We stand before Rev. Dick Leonard from the Unitarian Church of All Souls, the music has stopped, and the ceremony begins.

"We are gathered together to unite this man and this woman in marriage, which is an institution founded in nature, ordained by the state, sanctioned by church and synagogue, and made honorable by the faithful keeping of good men and women in all ages. It is, therefore, not by any to be entered into unadvisedly or lightly, but discreetly, advisedly, and with due reverence. This celebration is the outward token of a sacred and inward union of hearts, which institutions may bless and the state make legal, but which neither can create, a union created by your loving purpose and kept by your abiding will. Into this estate these two persons come to be united."

"Is it in this spirit and for this purpose that you have come hither to be joined together?"

Ed and I respond, "It is."

"Do you, Ed, take Linda to be your wife, to love and to cherish, to honor and to comfort, in sickness or in health, in sorrow or in joy, in hardship or in ease, to have and to hold, from this day forth?"

Ed's voice cracks. He says, "I do."

"Do you, Linda, take Ed to be your husband, to love and to cherish, to honor and to comfort, in sickness or in health, in sorrow or in joy, in hardship or in ease, to have and to hold, from this day forth?"

"I do."

"May he who gives this ring and she who wears it abide in peace unto their life's end."

Ed takes my left hand in his two hands and slips a band of gold with fourteen tiny diamonds on my third finger.

"With this ring," he says, "I thee wed." His voice cracks; a tear rolls down his cheek. "And pledge thee my faithful love."

Holding Ed's left hand in mine, I repeat the same words and slip a band of gold on his third finger.

We join hands, gaze into each other's eyes, and from the writer Camus, we say in place of the words we asked be omitted, "Do not walk ahead of me, I may not follow; do not walk behind me, I may not lead. Just walk beside me and be my friend."

Reverend Leonard says, "Forasmuch as Ed and Linda have thus pledged themselves each to the other in the presence of this company, I do now, by virtue of the authority vested in me by the Church and by the State of New York, pronounce that they are husband and wife. May all that is good, beautiful, and true abide with you forever. Amen."

Honoring Jewish tradition and celebrating our union, Ed raises his foot and stomps a champagne glass wrapped in blue linen. He takes me into his arms and presses his lips to mine. It is our first kiss as man and wife. I feel a tear rolling down my cheek. If I touch my face, I can feel it still, and to this day, I have no idea whose tear it is. I look at Ed, his coal-colored eyes, I see his smile, and wiping my face, I think to myself, *He looks like an angel—my angel.*

- 6 -

REALITY

*It was one of those priceless moments when the
sunshine takes away all life's shadows.*

—Bill Clinton

It is 7:30 a.m., December 31, 2003. It is a frigid snowy morning, and I am in Grace Medical Center gazing numbly out a fifth-floor window. In the snowy distance, a snowplow lumbers in and out of view, clearing a path to a parking lot for slow-moving, snow-covered cars. Bundled people trudge the newly shoveled sidewalk to the hospital entrance below, seemingly at my feet, and disappear through revolving glass doors, leaving a trail of footprints filling fast with snow. The sky is a swirling sea of white, and the only sounds are that of a bell and a sudden burst of chatter followed by a pregnant hush from outside Ed's room—a signal an elevator down the hall has arrived and departed. Ed lies tucked neatly into a bed of white linen. A cup of coffee sits on a tray table stretched across the bed before him. He reads *Time* magazine. I count snowflakes. This is one ugly misery-memory moment, the beginning of many, etched in the landscape of my brain, since learning my husband is ill. It is as if the proverbial elephant has stepped into my life and I am helpless to usher him out. As we sit and contemplate the present, we await results for Ed's blood test, CA-19-9, a tumor marker for a substance produced because of cancer, and the battery of other tests performed over the course of the last two weeks. We need to know what that mysterious lump on Ed's neck is. In a little while, a team of doctors will file through the door to Ed's room. Ed is quiet. I am quiet. We wait. For different reasons we are afraid.

Dr. C stands at Ed's side. Dr. C is Chinese. He is a short, stocky man who chuckles robustly after everything he says. He chats to the two men standing like bookends at his side. All three are dressed in white lab coats. Dr. C smiles. His two associates remain stern-faced. In a large voice, Dr. C says, "You have stage three adenocarcinoma!" He chuckles. "You have tumor!" He chuckles. "It is in the junction of your stomach. But not to worry." He chuckles. "I know about these things," he says. "We can help you here. You don't have to go noplace else. We take care of you right here." He chuckles.

Dr. C looks at his associates. He looks at Ed. Chuckling, he looks at me. I lower my eyes, pick up a pen, remove the paper napkin from under Ed's cup of coffee, and write. I write I want to slap Dr. C.

"Stop writing," Dr. C says. He places his hand over my pen. This time he does not chuckle.

Ed interrupts. "My wife is a writer," he says. "She writes everything down. She's writing a book."

"Not to worry," Dr. C chuckles. I feel his grasp tighten. "We shrink that tumor. We get your husband ready for surgery," he says. "We cut it out of him."

Unleashing his hold on my hand, he looks directly at Ed. "In no time you good as new, back on top of pretty wife." Dr. C chuckles. This time he looks at me. "It is not necessary to write everything down," he says. "We get this tumor."

I place my hand in my pocket and turn my eyes to the sea of snow falling softly out the window. The two men standing beside Dr. C stare out the window also. I wonder if they are counting snowflakes, too.

The doctor and his two associates file out of Ed's room, leaving Ed and me alone. In an instant I am out the door and racing down the hall, chasing after them. I call out to Dr. C, but he continues walking. One man turns to me, and I blurt out for him to please tell me if my husband is going to be all right. The man barely breaks stride and says, "Get your papers in order. Your husband is going to die." He says we all have to die someday. And then he chuckles.

I gulp a scream and watch as the man in long white lab coat turns and catches up to Dr. C and the other man. It is all I can do to take a breath. I feel like I am on board the *Titanic* and have just been given word the ship is going down.

I return to Ed's room, sit at his side facing the wintry view. He asks, what did the doctor say? I lie. I say I couldn't get his attention. I take his hand. I hold it warmly in mine. Looking into his face and tired eyes, I tell him everything is going to be all right. I say he is not going through this alone, that I am here for him, and that we will get through this together. My mind wanders. I rein it in. Whatever thoughts and fears I have inside me about Ed dying and what the doctor said, I put out of my head. Everything pales in comparison to what lies before my beloved husband. Everything. For a long while we just sit there staring at the sky, counting snowflakes. We hold each other close. I tell Ed I love him. He tells me he loves me back. We kiss. It's a brief kiss. Hardly any kiss at all. Then, in typical Ed fashion, he tells me to go home and get the checkbook. He says, "I need to teach you a few things about running the household and paying the bills."

- 7 -

MOMENTS

*Live in the now, as often as you can,
a breath here, a moment there.*

—Anne Lamott

To prepare Ed for surgery, it is mandatory to reduce his tumor. Dr. C prescribes six treatments of chemo therapy to do the job.

"Maybe one more," Dr. C says with a chuckle.

Upon completion of the six or more chemo treatments, Ed is promised he will be a candidate for surgery.

When Dr. C relays this information to Ed and me, he waves one hand like a magician pulling a rabbit out of a hat and promises the tumor can be "cut out" at that time. A surgery date of March 12, 2004 at Hunter Memorial in Manhattan is scheduled.

Dr. C explains that the chemo treatments will be administered at Grace Medical Center, thus eliminating the need to travel into the city. We are given instructions—Ed will receive the chemo therapy, and I will be his caregiver. We are told that due to Ed's aggressive cancer, treatments must be administered in three week intervals, and, as if chatting about the weather, a chuckling Dr. C further explains each treatment will last 96 hours, consist of pumping chemicals,

Fluorouracil (a platinum drug more commonly referred to as 5-FU), Cisplatin, and Paclitaxel, out a plastic box, through a plastic tube, into a port surgically implanted in Ed's chest—think plastic baggy attached to square blue box with blinking laser lights hanging off a steel pole on wheels—connected to a straw hanging out a necklace of tubing in Ed's chest. And, at the end of each treatment, Ed can go home and get on with his normal duties, even return to work, if he so desires.

Of the three chemicals pumped into Ed, 5-FU was the most toxic. So radioactive is Fluorouracil that it must be covered to protect it from sunlight and prevent it from leaking radiation. The nurse administering the drug wore gloves. (After Ed's death, some years later, I read this chemical was so high in toxicity and so resistant to cancerous tumors, it prompted discovery of two less-toxic platinum and more effective drugs and was no longer used to fight cancer.) As far as I was concerned, the aggressive cancer Ed had and at the late stage it had been discovered, no matter what chemotherapy was prescribed, it was all a veiled attempt to make it look like something could be done to save his life. The truth is that the chemo prescribed for Ed, with all its packaged toxic waste, was useless. What it succeeded in doing was weakening an already weakened immune system in a seriously ill man, prolonging suffering, and sucking money out of a wallet. Ed had suffered a blood clot in his jugular. By any account, based on the CA-19-9 blood test given to make his diagnosis, Ed still standing and walking around was a huge miracle. That he was able to actively participate in his care was a double miracle, and he was lucky to be alive and functioning as well as he did. I liken the process of trying to save Ed's life with chemotherapy to sticking a thumb in a New Orleans dike during Hurricane Katrina. Ed was a walking, talking dead man. I knew it, so did Ed. But buoyed and filled with hope by what his doctor had told him, he accepted wholeheartedly that in order to survive he must fight the good fight, and if drinking poison would win the war against his cancer, well, by golly, bring it on. Ed, goddammit, was determined to do it. Why not? A chuckling Dr. C made it sound simple as eating angel food cake. I knew better. My father died of cancer. My mother died of cancer. My two best girlfriends died of cancer. Even my dog Sammy died of cancer. In every instance, the cancer had been discovered too late. Common sense dictated a different strategy should have been taken.

The diagnosis of esophageal cancer was a lot to process for Ed and me, and I realized at the very start, the treatment prescribed to cure Ed was educated guesswork gleaned from a cookbook of experimental drugs. Ed's tumor was six centimeters and located in the junction of his esophagus and stomach. Know here and now, Ed did not smoke, and he did not drink. How he got the cancer that riddled his body, I have no idea. Nobody does. The operation recommended to save his life was to have the surgeon cut out a portion of his stomach, cut out the tumor, cut away a portion of his esophagus, and reconnect the shortened piece of esophagus to the reduced stomach, making Ed's stomach the size of a grapefruit and his esophagus as short as a string bean. At best, the life-saving surgery would restrict Ed's diet, mandate he sleep in an upright position the rest of his life, possibly extend his life two to five years—maybe maybe maybe—and it carried a survival rate of 30 percent. Maybe.

Ed, ever the believer that the glass was half full, believing every word Dr. C said, elected immediately to have the chemotherapy and asked me to support his decision. I sucked air, gritted my teeth, and did. With my whole heart and entire soul, and against and despite my better judgment, I supported Ed's decision and rooted for the home team through the horror of two 96-hour chemo treatments. As toxic chemicals coursed through Ed's veins, snuffing out his immune system, one teensy cell at a time, making him sick sicker sickest, weak weaker weakest, I sat ringside, captive audience, smiling hard, and cheering Ed on. The whole time, with each drip of the IV, I grew more suspicious of the American Medical Association and Dr. C. With each hiccup, gag, and cough Ed made, I watched him put up the good fight and endure tremendous suffering. But independent of Ed, and much to the chagrin of Dr. C, I asked hard questions and demanded honest answers. They didn't come, so on my own I began to research Ed's cancer. Along with relatives, personal friends in the medical profession, and the internet, I found out what Dr. C would not tell me, and what Ed's family physician for more than five years, Dr. O, had missed.

On January 1, 2004, at the nurses' station, the first day of Ed's first chemo treatment, I asked Dr. C why the CA-19-9 tumor marker blood test used to diagnose my husband's cancer, since it is so dependable and reliable, was not used as a preventative for cancer for everyone, like a Pap smear, for example. The doctor told me I was concerning myself with the wrong thing and not to concern myself with the stuff on the internet. He told me those studies are more than five years old. I refused to listen. The reason, I discovered in my research, and as every doctor knows, is that by the time a cancer shows up in a CA-19-9 blood test, it is already too late to save the patient, which was positively certainly definitely the case with Ed. My next question is why any doctor would prescribe for a man in Ed's condition, six, possibly seven, debilitating, life-threatening chemo treatments, knowing it was already too late to save his life.

On my own, I came to the conclusion back then and believe the same holds true today, that here in the United States, it is no secret that cancer is big business. I have learned that the pharmaceutical companies supplying the chemo drugs rule the American Medical Association, making chemo a billion-dollar business, along with some of the doctors who prescribe it, preying on desperate people, and promoting it. My stance is, and continues to be, regarding Ed's diagnosis, why give hope where none existed?

On the evening of December 31, 2003, after Ed had been diagnosed, after I had run home and returned with the checkbook, and after a small box called a port, had been surgically implanted in Ed's chest, Ed was whisked from his room on the fifth floor into a waiting elevator down the hall and escorted to a semiprivate room on the seventh floor. The seventh floor is the cancer ward. It is the same floor where my mother died in 1978, and the place I privately refer to as God's waiting room. Toting Ed's overnight bag and trailing two orderlies guiding Ed's stretcher, I choked back tears, passing the parade of desperately ill patients languishing in the hall, each attached to a piece of luggage pumping chemo into their bodies. Perception is reality and my reality was the kick-in-the-belly knowledge my husband was terminally ill and there was not a damn thing I could do about it. As we entered the dim room at the far end of the hall, the dirge from Tennyson's Charge of the Light Brigade, *Into the valley of death ...* flooded my brain.

It is January 8, 2004. We are home from the hospital. Ed's first chemo treatment is finished. He is nauseous, his complexion is ashen, and his gait is clumsy. When I try to take his arm to steady and help him into the car, he snaps at me. He says, leave me alone. He says, I am not an invalid. He says, stop babying me. In the garage at our townhome, he stumbles out of the car, catches his fall, staggers into the den, and hugs the doorway. He pants like a dog in hot weather, and outside the temperature is 29 degrees Fahrenheit. As I look into Ed's face, I recall the doctor's chilling words *get your papers in order*, my mother's and father's suffering, and I know this is the beginning of Ed's terrible horrible ugly nightmare. It hits me—I will live to bury this man.

Ed is tucked neatly in bed. A TV clicker rests in the palm of one hand, and a paper cup filled with apple juice is held in the other. I am in the kitchen preparing lunch, tuna on white bread, Ed's favorite, with teensy chopped bits of onion, a quartered half-sour Claussen pickle, and a bowl of Lipton chicken soup, the only soup Ed will eat. At any moment, the visiting nurse will arrive. This woman will instruct me how to care for Ed.

A large cardboard box of supplies delivered the day before hugs the front door. Inside is one week's supply of saline solution.

The nurse arrives, sits at the kitchen table, fingers a large, black loose-leaf book. She opens to a tab. This is where you enter the date, she says, pointing. Here is where you enter the amount; she points again. Still pointing, she says to keep the saline solution in the refrigerator until ready to use, warm it in the microwave or a pan of warm water before giving it. You don't want to give it to him cold, she says. The nurse asks where we will go if Indian Point has a problem and if there is an evacuation. Indian Point is located in Buchanan, twenty-something miles north of Hartsdale. The concern is that the nuclear power plant will have a meltdown—think China syndrome—and the nurse needs to put something in writing for her records, some plan of action that Ed and I will perform in case of emergency.

I do not answer the nurse. Considering the bleak outlook given me by doctors and professionals, and what I have learned on the internet, I just sit there laughing heartily to myself.

The nurse says, "I need an answer." She says, "I must have a contact name and a telephone number."

I look the nurse dead in the eye. I say, "We are going no place." I say, "If a bomb drops and we are commanded to evacuate, Ed and I will stay put." I say, "We can't run from a cancer; it is nuts to think we can outrun a plume."

For a long time the nurse fingers her pen. She stares at the open page in her loose-leaf. After a short pause, she says, "I'll just write that you're going to your brother's in Connecticut."

The day wears on. I have been taught how to hydrate Ed, how to work the necklace of tubing hanging out the box inserted in his chest, how to attach the bag of saline solution to a steel pole on wheels, and how to monitor the number of drips per second through the tube. Not too fast. Not too slow. I am petrified. I am taught how to give a subcutaneous injection, a shot in the belly, how to prepare a clean area in which to work and gather materials, and how to draw medication from an ampule or vial and inject it into Ed. With the visiting nurse looking over my shoulder, I practice on a paper napkin, flicking the syringe for air bubbles. I am scared I will kill my husband if I make a mistake.

A Gift of Love

It is Monday, January 19, 2004. Martin Luther King Day. Outside the weather is frigid. Westchester County is covered in snow. Due to the holiday, there is no mail delivery, and banks and schools are closed. Youngsters trudge snow-covered sidewalks, and teens drive slushy side roads to malls and movie theaters to do all the fun things kids do on winter break.

Ed and I are on our way to A&P, our local grocery store, located less than a mile from our townhouse. Ed insists on taking me. He says he'll drive. His Camry is parked in our attached two-car garage alongside my Corolla. Bundled in boots, warm coats, woolen scarves, hats, gloves, and mittens, we get in the car and buckle up. Ed pushes the garage door button clipped to the visor over his head, and as the door creeps open and glides into the roof above us, he turns the key in the ignition and throws the gearshift into reverse. Backing out onto the crusted snowy driveway, the car wheels bite into the frozen path, making crunch-crunch sounds that echo inside the cold car. As we make our way past the gatehouse leading into our community and the entrance of Stone Oaks Drive to Hartsdale Road and the plowed parking lot around the corner, we are quiet; each of us lost in our own private sea of thoughts. The Camry parked and our hands clasped firmly together, we enter the grocery store. Ed pushes a carriage grabbed from the bank of carriages located at the front entrance. Passing fresh bananas, heads of romaine lettuce, and glass-encased freshly cut flowers, we walk the aisles, stopping along the way to fill our cart with things we need. At the dairy case, I reach for a container of milk and tub of butter. Ed is free to shop on his own.

"Do we need Swiss cheese?" he asks, shaking a small see-through envelope in the air.

I shake my head. Slowly, I push the cart down the canned goods aisle. From the corner of my eye, I see Ed return the package to the display hook. Trying not to stare, I notice Ed's hand tremble. He misses his mark. He tries again. Again he misses. His third try, the slotted bag slips uneasily over and around the hook. There is a pause, as if Ed is deep in thought. He looks in my direction, and I am certain he is checking to see if I have noticed. My eyes dart away. Ed looks old, very old. His first chemo treatment has puffed his face, chubbied his fingers, and paunched his belly. It is the first time in our years together that I see my Ed a doddering old man on the threshold of death.

At the checkout, the belt carries our groceries, and the cashier rings each item. When she is finished, the register shows a total of $68.48. Ed reaches a clumsy hand into his side pants pocket. It gets stuck, and for a moment, he struggles to pull it free. Money clip in hand, he counts two twenties and one ten into the fuzzy-haired woman's palm. He stops, as if to take a breath. He stares at the paper money he just counted, points a fat finger over each lonely bill, and stops. There is a pause, and the cashier shakes her hand impatiently. Ed reaches for his money clip once more and removes three fives, and three singles, placing them on top of the other bills in the anxious woman's hand. Reaching into his other pocket with his other chubby hand, he holds out a clutch of loose change. His hand trembles as he smoothes one puffy finger over four dimes, one nickel, and three pennies. Working to pinch two fat fingers together, he manages to pick each coin out of the palm of his open hand and places them into the outstretched palm of the restless cashier's open hand.

In an instant, the woman balls her hand, clasping the bills and loose change in a tight fist. The money drawer open, without counting, she opens her hand, plops the bills and loose change into each appropriate slot, rips the paper receipt from the register, punches it into the palm of Ed's shaking hand, and, with her right hip, slams the register drawer shut, moving her hand immediately to the next customer's groceries piled on the belt in front of me.

Ed takes hold of our cart, and heads to the electric door. *S-l-o-w-l-y.* At the same time, canned goods slide by me in fast forward motion, and I feel the steel bow of a waiting customer's grocery cart in the small of my back through the padded lining of my winter coat.

"Want me to push?"

"No."

In the snow-covered parking lot, new snow swirls the frosted air. It powders a layer of snow over ice, dims visibility, and blankets parked cars. The invisible layer of ice lurking beneath the falling snow causes the wheels of the grocery cart Ed pushes to slide and slip. He struggles to maintain balance and keep the cart from tipping over while impatient drivers scouring the lot for empty parking spaces weave perilously close. They beep their horns at Ed, and through their front windows and salting air, I read their lips. They are cursing at Ed. In the freezing cold, a woman winds down the window of her Lexus and yells, "Get the fuck out of my way." I want to reach out, grab the cart from Ed's hands, and scream my guts out at this woman. I want to rescue Ed, but as with his impending death, I realize there is nothing I can do. I am a captive audience. I am helpless as a newborn kitten, knowing if I say anything, it will hurt Ed's feelings, and if I don't say anything, I hurt mine. Damned if I do, damned if I don't, I embrace silence and watch the whole ugly scene unfold before my crying eyes, while Ed, seemingly unaffected by the strange woman's behavior, remains calm as an evening lake, battling the icy elements, unyielding drivers, and heinous disease that ravages his body. Numbly, I watch as he wheels the loaded cart to his Camry and empties it, one bag at a time, into the open trunk. His eyes meet mine, and there it is, greeting me in radiant splendor, his warm, embraceable smile. Ed closes the trunk gently, glances over at me once again, and winks.

How does he do it? I wonder. *And when will he break?*

On the short drive home, Ed asks, How's your writing going? He asks, What are you reading? I say I just finished Annie Dillard's book on writing. I say I didn't know this woman was a Pulitzer Prize winner. I say I didn't know she's written ten books. I take a breath, stare out the side window at the lone grocery cart sitting idly in the open space we just pulled out of, and say I can't imagine writing anything like that. I tell Ed I feel so intimidated. He smiles and asks me what it is I am writing. At the moment I am on assignment for

Westchester Parent magazine; my editor, Renée Cho, has assigned me an interview.

"I have to do an interview with Ivey Levy," I say.

"Who is Ivey Levy?"

"Ivey is a foodie. She cooks. She gives tips on how to organize a kitchen."

I tell Ed that more than anything in the world I want to write a book and present it to him. Ed knows my passion to write a book. I have told him many times. He is an avid reader, polishing off paperback novels in rapid-fire succession, sometimes two a week. He travels more than one hundred thousand miles a year on business and says he likes to fill his brain with mindless reading, as he calls it—a necessary respite from a demanding job—while on board an airplane traveling to and from a business trip. Ed says he likes that he can pick up a paperback, carry it around with him easily, open it, read it, stop at any page, and not have to reread several pages to get back into the story when he picks it up again. With the progression of Ed's illness and his working from home, I notice Ed's thirst for paperback novels increases. Finished paperbacks are piled knee-high in the corner of our den, and daily the stack grows taller and wider. At the traffic light, I touch Ed's hand.

"Someday," I say, "I want to write a book and dedicate it to you. I want to make you proud of me."

Ed closes his gloved hand over mine and smiles. "Not to worry," he says. "You already have."

The light changes red to green, and with one hand on the steering wheel, the other clasping mine, Ed drives back to Stone Oaks Drive.

Ed's cancer arrived on little fog feet and changed our lives forever. The cough, the only symptom Ed exhibited prior to the swelling on his neck, was diagnosed three years earlier by Dr. O as asthma. Dr. O prescribed an inhaler, some hand-held yellow-and-orange plastic device Ed squirted into his mouth while holding his breath whenever the cough came. For more than one year, maybe longer, the cough increased in intensity, and Ed sucked on that silly plastic thing, believing the whole time it was curing what ailed him. Now, in the shadow of death, we know for certain it was cancer that made that cough, and not asthma. I am angry with Ed's doctor. I want to scream and rail against the world at the injustice of it all; and there stands Ed, my beloved husband, with an inoperable tumor, stage three adenocarcinoma, sprouting blood clots in his jugular vein, and not complaining. He isn't saying one damn bad word about the doctor, the mistake, or about the whole damn ugly thing.

About the same time as Ed's diagnosis, old man winter rolls in. The weatherman might just as well have gone away and left one recorded message: *Windy, cold, snowy, sleet and ice—today, tomorrow, and forever after that.* The weather, like Ed's cancer, never gets better; it just gets worse. As Ed's cancer blisters his insides, the wind gets windier, cold grows colder, and the snow, snowier. One cold morning, after a long, hard night of tending to Ed's litany of misery, bleary-eyed and fighting a good cry, I drag myself out of bed and stagger into the bathroom. Covered in a blanket of white, the high hillside out the back of our townhome reflects warm sunlight. It splashes through the windows of our bedroom and casts willowy naked tree limb shadows on rosebud-papered walls. White light filters through the open bathroom door, creating a looking-glass scene. Aglow in an aura of morning sunlight and poised over the sink, staring at his reflection, Ed rubs his head and blurts, "I'm bald!"

Ed is bald, all right, bald as a bowling ball. There isn't a hair on his shiny white head, his puffy fat face, china-white cheeks, underarms, forearms, or legs. Even his pubic hair has disappeared. It is as if a giant art eraser has rubbed out each strand of hair on his body, right down to the follicle. Ed's hair loss, of course, is a direct result of his first ninety-six-hour, in-hospital, three-chemical, toxic chemo treatment, administered less than two weeks earlier at Grace Medical Center. A halo of fatigue circles Ed's eyes, making them seem larger, his nose pointier. His complexion is gray and matted as fur on a dead squirrel. I observe his worried expression reflected in the mirrored glass and divert my eyes. Sucking in a deep breath, my brain cruises for something kind and gentle to say.

"Look at me," Ed says. "I have no hair." His voice cracks.

I rub my eyes, making myself look like I am rubbing sleep from them, but really I am pushing away tears.

"I look like a turtle."

I start to cry. "No, you don't," I say. I say, "You look beautiful." I say, "You are beautiful." Then I fall into Ed's arms and bury my face in the crook of his shoulder and sob. The words *you are my husband* and *I love you* spring from my melting heart. "You look beautiful," I say. I say it over and over until Ed says, "Linda Please, don't cry."

- 8 -

CHANGE

But I think one of the most important things in life is to be open-minded and to be open-minded for change.

—Jenna Bush Hager

As the reality of Ed's advancing cancer takes hold of our lives, we shutter our world. Round-trip tickets to Hong Kong are returned to the travel agency. Next year's vacation to St. Maarten is canceled. We call friends and family members only when absolutely necessary. Dinner invitations are politely declined, and we no longer invite guests for dinner. There is little time to socialize. We stop talking about the cancer and the chemo. We conserve energy and live in the moment, treasuring fleeting seconds. I meditate, Ed watches television. He reads, I write. We sit in bookstores and coffee shops, and, because Ed is concerned for his appearance, we travel to out-of-the-way diners to sit anonymously on those days we choose to leave the house. On clear crisp days, we go to Rye Beach and stroll the boardwalk. It is freezing cold, and we do not care. We make a conscious decision to be with just each other. Our privacy is paramount. Familiar faces become an intrusion. Well-meaning friends, extended family members, and especially friendly neighbors, in our eyes, have become creepy curiosity seekers. Unintentionally, they make our lives difficult, asking questions we do not have answers for and choose to ignore when we do. We pass our time telling silly knock-knock jokes, recalling embarrassing moments, and vowing not to disagree or argue about anything ever again. We make plans to see a movie; tomorrow, we say, because tomorrow is all we got. *Maybe.*

With each passing day, Ed grows more frail, weak as water. He looks breakable. His white blood count is dangerously low, and doctors are concerned about infection. I tell Ed to stay inside, to please rest. I say I will carry the garbage from the kitchen to the outside shed. I can do this, I say, scooting out the door. Don't worry, I'll be all right, I say. Dressed in robe and slippers, Ed stands guard in the doorway in the glow of our warm townhome, watching me walk out the door into the frigid air. In a moment my feet slip and slide out from under me, and I fall. The white plastic garbage bag I carry breaks loose from my grip, tears open as it hits the jagged, ice-encrusted rocky path, and spews a trail of banana peels, orange rinds, coffee grounds, soiled paper napkins, and empty plastic saline bags to the driveway and into the street. Ed watches me crawl in the ice and snow on my hands and knees, scooping the gooey mess in ungloved hands. He sees me slip and slide, up and down the icy path. My short walk from front door to shed located directly in front of our townhome has turned Kafkaesque. I get to the shed, and the latch is frozen shut. I cannot work it free. Ed watches through the window of the storm door as, clinging to raw trash, my feet slipping out from under me, I fight the feisty lock until it releases; the whole time I am spilling garbage in snow, and my feet are wishing for a bag of rock salt. Covered in the cloak of an open shed door, I work the trash pail cover free. It is as frozen as the latch, but I breathe a sigh of relief; I am out of Ed's view. I make it happen—dump the snow-laced mess into the pail and scour the entry path for more garbage, used tissues, an empty peanut butter jar, lollipop wrappers, ice cream and bread wrappers. My chore complete, I slam the shed door shut, making certain the frozen latch catches. When I look up again, I see my husband standing in the doorway, making a smile at me. His eyes are wet. This time it is he who fights back tears. I realize they are at the sight of me doing work he usually does, and it is as painful for him to watch me spill trash in the snow and say nothing as it is for me to watch him fight a grocery cart in an A&P parking lot on a cold winter day. It is all just too much too soon for either of us to process.

Judy called yesterday. Judy is Ed's big sister. Judy called yesterday, the day before yesterday, and the day before that. Today the telephone rings. It is eight o'clock a.m. I am standing over the kitchen sink, washing dishes. Ed is in the den, reading the morning paper. Wrapped in his lime green terry cloth robe, Ed picks up the telephone. I hear him say hi to Judy. I turn the water off. I listen.

'I didn't mean to be so short with you yesterday. It's just that calling us every day is painful. It's hard on me. It's hard on Linda. We don't need to talk about it over and over. When we do, it brings up painful memories. I still have more chemo to go through. Then there's the operation. I'm not looking forward to that. It's hard when the office and everyone calls constantly. We'll call you in a couple of days. ... I'm losing my hair. ... Yes, I know it'll grow back."

Wednesday arrives—or is it Thursday? The garbage men are here. Oh, yes, it is Thursday, and it is the end of the month. I think. I am so weary and confused from caring for and worrying about Ed, I carry a notebook and pen everywhere I go to jot down the simplest of tasks I must remember to do to take care of him. While I create a document on the computer listing Ed's prescriptions and how often to take each pill, Ed hovers over my shoulder, directing my fingers. Names of pills are so long and confusing that we simply dub them blue, pink, yellow, orange, purple, round white, fat white, and chunky white. Make it five columns, Ed says. No, make it six. He grabs my hand. He says to make it landscape, not portrait. Do it over. This is wrong.

He fusses when the page doesn't print out exactly the way he wants it. He says to make a label for this column. He points and says this column is for morning pills. He says to make sure I get the dosage right. Here, he says, let me check it. Look, he says, you missed this. He points again. The blue pill, he says, is taken three times a day, not two. The white one, he says, and yellow and orange ones are twice a day: morning and just before I go to bed. He points a pale, puffed finger at the paper's edge. Here, he says, put a box here.

I don't mind he's proofing every word I type as I type it. I don't mind he's breathing down my neck. For some strange reason, it feels wonderful. I understand. It is a necessary distraction for us both, and it makes Ed feel useful and takes his mind off dying. If nothing else, it gives Ed something to boss about and someone to boss. In the big picture, it really doesn't matter how I feel. For now, for Ed, for the sakes of our sanity, whatever day it is, it is just another cold, windy, snowy, Ed-got-a-cancer, winter day, and we're just trying to get through it.

Outside, the earth is a blanket of white. Snow is falling. I get into the driver's seat of my Corolla, back out of the garage, and head to the A&P. Inside, Ed lies resting peacefully in our upstairs bedroom. The only sounds are that of the TV turned down low and the drip drop drip of an IV pumping a see-through bag of saline attached to a pole on wheels through clear plastic tubing into the port in Ed's chest. We're out of lollipops. We've got no more Ritz crackers, and the box containing packets of Lipton chicken noodle soup mix is empty. The chemo treatment has hideous side effects, and for three weeks now, Ed's been living them. Ed needs hard sucking candy to relieve the metallic taste in his mouth from the platinum chemo drug that trickled through his veins. He needs chicken soup to provide nourishment. He needs ginger ale to stay hydrated. And we're out of Froot Loops, Ed's favorite breakfast cereal. Since Ed's chemo treatment, he is unable to eat food without gagging and throwing up. Sugary sweet Froot Loops in a bowl splashed in whole milk masks the nauseating metal-pipe taste that permeates Ed's mouth, tongue, and lips. It is the only food he is able to tolerate. Today, this day, I am alone in my mission to shop for groceries. For maybe the first time ever, Ed is not driving me to the grocery store, our weekly ritual since we got married. It feels odd and the message *Most likely it will never happen again* hits hard. The entire time I am away from the house, my mind is on my sick husband. The ground is cold. Thick snowflakes rain out of the sky, powder the roof and front and rear windows of my Corolla, and make side roads risky and dangerous. Windshield wipers swishing furiously, I pull into the A&P lot and park my car. Dodging fat snowflakes and dashing for the store entrance, I grab a cart and race the aisles for each item. Flash fast, I am out of the store, back to the Corolla, hastily brushing snow off the roof, front, side, and rear widows and turning a key in the ignition. On the short drive back to Stone Oaks Drive, my mind plays a litany of worst-case scenarios: *What if Ed dies? What if I'm not there when it happens?*

Caring for Ed requires my undivided, twenty-four-hours-a-day attention, and he hates that. Ed is accustomed to caring lovingly for me—not the other way around; and lately, sometimes, he behaves like an unruly child, insisting he can do everything himself, even when he can't. The hardest part about caring for Ed is not letting on that he is no longer capable of caring for himself. By day I concern myself with overnight hospital stays, visiting hours, doctors' appointments, prescriptions to be filled, prescriptions to be picked up, what needle to administer to Ed, and where to administer it. I scrub bathroom and kitchen floors until they gleam brightly in the dark, and I keep germs at bay of well-meaning inquisitive neighbors, friends, business associates, and family members. Home from the grocery store, I drop my flimsy plastic grocery bags filled with Ed items onto the entry hall floor and tiptoe up the stairs to check on Ed. Passing the TV on the dresser opposite the foot of our bed, I make my way to Ed's bedside, lean close to his face, and check for breath. I breathe a sigh of relief. I am so grateful for breath. Ed's eyes are closed, but a slight purring sound emanates from his lips and nose as his chest rises and falls. It is a good sound. Tenderly, I check his IV for air bubbles and leaks, running two fingers along the clear plastic tube from the top of the IV bag to the necklace of clips hanging out his port. Ed is pale, his body limp as a thirsty dandelion. It hurts deeply to look at him. So painful is that vision, I turn away and stare out the window at the snow-covered rock mountain looming large before me. I am lost in a sea of depressing thoughts, while a female cardinal pecks snow, her strange beak popping the glistening white landscape. For the longest time, I just stand there, my arms hanging like two dead rabbits at my sides, fighting the urge to cry.

Ed's hand. It touches mine.

"Are you all right?"

"I didn't know you were awake," I say. I clasp his hand with both of mine. No words are spoken. Except for the drip drop drip of his IV, we share silence. Bad as I feel for me, I feel worse for Ed. My beloved husband is dying, and the best I can offer is a rubber-banded bouquet of lollipops and a giant box of Kellogg's Froot Loops.

"Yeah," I say, my eyes fixed on the pale red bird making V prints with her feet in the snow. I don't want to admit to Ed what the doctors have told me, what I have read on the internet, what his doctor brother-in-law, Jim, has shared, and the hopelessness I feel knowing that in a little while he will be dead. I will be alone. And I am scared. I am wishing and hoping and praying for Ed with all my heart to please get well, but my simple brain tells me it's not going to happen. The doctors have told me this, Dr. Jim has said it, and I have read it. I just can't bear to tell Ed.

"Yeah," I say, again.

Ed's hand grasps mine. I gulp. I have never said an untrue word to my husband, nor he to me, that I know of, during our marriage, but the lie I have just told is huge. It is huge as the snow-covered hard rock mountain looming large through the bedroom window staring back at me. My husband is alive. He is not dead, not yet. And I miss him. I miss him terribly. Instead of saying words of truth out loud, I hold them inside me. I fight crying in front of Ed, but I am not good at hiding my feelings. One lone tear trickles down my cheek. My face might just as well be made of cellophane. Ed is quiet. I go into the bathroom and wash it. I return downstairs and put the groceries away.

Ed rests in a bed of white linen, and I sit by his blanketed side, scribbling in a spiral notebook, doing writing practice. I am pondering my future. I write, "I want Ed to tell me what to do after he is"—I stumble, I cannot write the "d word." Yet. I want Ed to tell me where to live after he dies. I want my beautiful, devoted husband, the man I have spent the last seventeen years of my life with, whom I love deeply and passionately, to make everything all better. I know nothing is forever—not summer vacations, childhood, or my precious marriage—and I know we all must die someday, but knowing it and living it is so damn hard and so damn ugly. I say it here and now, no one can say for certain how they will handle the death of their loved one, not until it happens to them, not until it is their beloved spouse dying in the bed next to them.

Ed was nine years older than I. His dream was the simple dream, the one every traditional American dares to dream: work hard, live frugally, budget, save, scrimp, and go without, postponing living life to its fullest, until retirement. The memory of Ed looking forward to retirement, asking me for six years more and promising that we'll buy a little house back in 1998 when we first moved into Hartsdale, filled me. And now it is six years later, and pressed into the bed of white linen and covered in his mother's rose-stitched afghan, is Ed. Dying. I clasp his hand and try to make sense of it all, realizing none of it will happen, and the wall-sized mirror hanging over my dresser facing the foot of our bed captures our pitiful image. Ed knows it; I know it; and even Izzy the dog, curled round as a button at the foot of our bed, knows it. I am just the only one in the house not good at concealing feelings.

- 9 -

LIMBO

And don't think too much.

—George L. Griffin III, my son

It is a frigid Tuesday in February, and Ed is home from his second chemo treatment, twice as sick as with the first one. During the night he awakens, clutches his stomach, and races for the bathroom. When I get up to check on him, I find him on his knees, hugging the toilet bowl. It is 2:30 in the morning, and he is throwing up. When he finishes, he fills a paper cup with flat ginger ale from the opened can resting on the counter and washes down an Ativan, a pill for nausea. When he is back in bed, tucked into covers around and over him, I kiss his sweating brow and think all is well. I make my way around to my side of the bed and slip under the covers. I fall asleep. In a short while I am awakened. Ed has hiccups. For thirty minutes, by the tick of the glow-in-the-dark numbers emanating the alarm clock on my nightstand, Ed rocks the bed with earth-shaking hiccups. Giant, galloping hiccups. Think Volkswagen bouncing off a cliff. It is 3:45 in the morning, and I can't take another minute. Naked and frightened, I limp out of the bedroom and slink down the carpeted stairs. Standing in the darkness, I gaze out the sliding glass doors into the base of the looming snow-covered rock wedged tightly behind our wooden deck and the great outdoor wintry wonderland. Clorox white and glistening in the half of a golden moon, icicles, dripped frozen, hang ominously from the eaves of the roof and cast eerie shadows on the snow-white mountain wall. Shivering, I embrace myself and begin to realize all the things I love about my beloved Ed, and all the things about him that I will miss when he is gone. Thoughts of his impending death flood my brain, and into the still, frozen night, I whisper words to the lying, dying, hiccupping man in the room directly above me.

I will miss the thump-thump beat of your heart. I will miss your body sleeping beside me. I will miss the warmth of your breath on the nape of my neck and your soapy fresh scent after a morning shower. I will miss your handsome face pressed softly to mine. I will miss your coal-colored eyes, soft lips, voice, and radiant smile. I will miss hearing words: Linda Please. Honey, I'm home, what's for dinner? I love you. I did stupid. *And* Pay no attention to my sister, Judy, my sister Judy is crazy. *Yes, I will miss you, Ed. I will miss you every day for the rest of my life.*

It is the following evening. Ed complains his throat feels like he has just gulped a lit match. He says he cannot swallow. He says his throat burns like fire. He gasps for breath and screams. It is a Friday night, and I dial Dr. C's office. I get his answering service, and I am told the good doctor has left for the day. I say my husband needs help, and I don't know what to do. I describe Ed's symptoms. I say I am frightened. The answering service takes my name and number. It tells me to wait by the phone for the on-call physician to call me back. The on-call doctor telephones, and when he hears what is happening with Ed, he instructs me to take Ed to the emergency room, immediately. He says he will meet us there. We arrive and Ed is placed on a stretcher and wheeled into a curtained examination room. After Ed is examined, the doctor recommends Ed be admitted for observation and treatment for pain. I stand in the hall listening to Ed plead for a painkiller—no, make that *beg* for a painkiller. He is hooked up to an IV and continues screaming loudly for something, anything to relieve his pain. The knot in my stomach grows tighter. I lean into the wall for support, put my face in my hands, and sob. My husband is writhing in pain, and, I am ashamed to admit, I secretly wish for a gun with two bullets to end our misery. The quiet man I call husband is carrying on so loudly his voice reverberates from the examination room and spills into the hall to the nurse's station twenty feet away. A nurse comes to me and asks if she can get me a glass of water. I grab onto her arm and say, "Can you please tell me when my husband will feel better?" Her smile turns upside down. She touches my shoulder. Quietly, she walks away. Nobody has answers to my questions, and if they do, they do not say.

The cancer ward on the seventh floor is out of beds, so a private room with a view of the familiar snow-covered parking lot is located on a different floor for Ed. He is sedated, hooked up to a morphine drip, and fully admitted. Two attendants navigate Ed's stretcher into an elevator, down a wide hall. I tag along, toting winter coats and purse, drying my eyes and wiping my nose on the sleeve of my sweater. Three hours later, Ed is resting peacefully. Pain-free and calm as an evening lake, we hold hands. Seeing Ed in that hospital bed swathed in a sea of white linen, cared for by nurses and doctors, I breathe an open sigh of relief. It feels good to see him comfortable, arms folded, hands clasped neatly in his lap, and resting peacefully. His grimace of pain gone, and pinkish glow returned, despite baldness, puffiness, and flaming sore throat, I confess, my husband looks good. Thank you, god, for morphine drip, I pray silently. By the light of a golden moon filtering through the uncurtained window, we sit and assure each other tomorrow will be a better day, because we believe truly the worst is behind us. We are so relaxed and fueled with hope and optimism, we talk about a trip to Costa Rica. I say, don't forget, I want to see a rain forest. Ed says, and don't forget Italy; I want to see where your grandparents came from. A nurse walks in. She remembers Ed from December, when he first arrived for tests. She gives him a warm welcome and hugs him. She says she is sorry to see him back so soon. The nurse with a caring smile winks at me, commenting hospital visiting hours are over, and adding sweetly not to worry. She says, "I have eye trouble, but it doesn't affect seeing my patients." A short time later I leave, promising Ed I'll see him in the morning. It is already after midnight, and I am exhausted.

Ed is resting peacefully when I walk out the door, and for the first time since his diagnosis and two chemo treatments, he looks healthy. A ray of hope glimmers in my brain, and I hold tight to it. I need hope, and this night of all nights, I latch onto the one moment that gives it. Anything that sees Ed make it peacefully through the night pain-free will do. I step out the elevator into the vacant lobby and think, *Hey, anything is possible.*

This night I sleep in an empty bed. There is no Ed by my side. It isn't the first time I sleep alone. Ed travels more than a hundred thousand miles a year on business. I have learned not to mind. It gives me precious time with Izzy, and, knowing it is temporary, pays the bills, and supports our lifestyle, it matters not at all. Sleeping without Ed this night is different. Everything is different since the cancer plowed into our lives, but this night I manage, because a flame of hope flickers in my dark heart.

A few hours later, it is time to return to the hospital. I shower, walk Izzy, hug Izzy, crate Izzy, and hurry back to Grace Medical Center to be with Ed. I stand at the doorway to Ed's room and see his oncologist, Dr. C, at his bedside. Our special nurse is gone; her shift has ended. Ed's cheeks are rosy, but lines that contorted his face when first we arrived have returned, dug deep in the furrow of his brow. An eerie sensation tells me something is not right. The doctor says Ed must leave the hospital immediately. He says, why did you rush Ed to the ER last night? He says, you need to take better care of your husband. He says, you need to take care of your husband at home. Ed is quiet and I tell the doctor Ed was in terrible pain last night and that I called him for help. I say, I was told you were out of the office. I say, it was your associate who directed me to bring Ed to the emergency room. I say, I did as I was told. I say, your service tried to contact you, and when they couldn't locate you, I was instructed to bring Ed to the emergency room. As soon as my words are out of my mouth, the doctor's eyes grow large as saucers. Then he storms out the room. I have no idea why. I start to cry. Ed touches my hand, but I will have none of it. The thought races through my brain that my husband is dying and his doctor is telling me I am doing a terrible job caring for him. It is a dagger in my heart, and the knot in my throat grows tighter. My hands tremble.

    I pack up Ed and his belongings, and with the help of aides, we are out the door. But before I leave, I steal a clean white sheet folded neatly at the foot of the bed. I have no idea why. A short time later we are in the car driving home to Hartsdale, a fistful of prescriptions folded and tucked inside my purse: a prescription for pain, a prescription for hiccups, a prescription for nausea, and a prescription for a tranquilizer to help Ed sleep. Leaving Ed in the front passenger seat of the Corolla with the engine running, I park in the CVS lot, dash inside, and drop off the prescriptions. I tell the pharmacist I will be back to pick them up. I race back to Ed and drive us home. I follow Ed up the stairs to our bedroom, at a safe distance so as not to upset him, but close enough to grab him should he stumble. I tuck him into bed. I dash back downstairs and return with a tray of hot chicken noodle soup, a half-dozen dry saltines, a paper cup filled with apple juice, a dish of raspberry Jell-O, and one grape Dum-Dum lollipop. I rush back down the stairs and out the door to pick up his prescriptions, the entire time thinking that I must take better care of my husband, that I am not doing a good job, and what a terrible caregiver I am. I feel like a sick nursery rhyme pig sticking its head out a car window, crying wee-wee-wee all the way home.

    It was time for Ed's third chemotherapy treatment. I was sitting in the kitchen staring at the refrigerator when Ed walked into the room. He said, "I have to make the appointment for my third chemo treatment." He said, "What should I do? I just don't know if I can take another treatment." I looked at Ed and shrugged. Tears spilled down my face. Ed admitted he had tremendous difficulty tolerating the treatments. "The first treatment," he said, "depleted my body and left me terribly weak." He took a breath. "The second treatment," he said, "made me worse off than the one before that. The thought of a third treatment and an additional three treatments, maybe one more, with no guarantee for recovery, well ..." He didn't go on. He was frightened, just as frightened as I was. Just the word *chemo* crippled my brain, and Ed's hard question landed like a rock on the rug. For a long while we were quiet.

We discussed the third treatment, possibly a fourth, fifth, and sixth, and side effects of each one based on what Ed had already experienced.

I turned to Ed "Don't worry about me," I said. "You do what's best for you. I'll be okay," I said. "I promise."

I lied.

Ed just stood there. For a long time he was silent. We both were. He stood silent. I sat fighting tears. I stopped staring at the refrigerator and turned my eyes to the brass knob on the bread drawer.

"If it's any consolation," I said, "you never had a chance. This disease is a bear."

Ed knelt at my side. He took my two hands from my face. Brushing tears from my cheeks, he looked into my eyes. For a long time we just stared at each other. Ed smiled. He wrapped his arms around me. I wrapped mine around him, and for the longest time, we held each other tight. I didn't want to think about tomorrow, or what the future was about to throw our way. Neither did Ed. Don't ask me how I knew what Ed was feeling. I just did.

Ed didn't do a third chemo treatment. It was his decision, and I supported it, wholeheartedly. After our talk, Ed contacted Hunter Memorial. "I want to live," he said. "I want the surgery. And I want it now."

He made an appointment with the surgeon, and seven days later we headed into Manhattan to keep it. Ed was weaker, his body more frail, his eyes sunk deeper in his head, and his complexion more charcoal. The evening before the appointment, he awakened with a pain in his side. As luck would have it, over the course of a week, Ed's body developed a kidney stone. Ed had a history of kidney stones, and he was up all night suffering through this latest attack. The following morning we made it to Hunter Memorial, Ed limping and leaning on me for support from the parking garage to the hospital the whole way. After the surgeon examined Ed, we received the news that no surgery could be performed until the stone was removed. This was not a good thing. Without Ed's third chemo treatment, the tumor was free to grow any which way it wanted, and any delay worsened the one-in-a trillion chance Ed had of beating it. Already a dangerous chunk of time had elapsed, but unless the kidney stone was removed, there could be no operation. Or so we were told. In a race for time, we contacted Ed's urologist in Harrison and explained to him what was happening, and Ed was scheduled for emergency surgery pronto. We drove directly from Hunter Memorial to United Hospital in Port Chester, where Ed was admitted that afternoon and operated on the following morning.

The kidney stone removed, Ed lay sedated and smiling broadly. He was filled with hope. My spirits lifted just seeing him happy and making future plans. We contacted Hunter Memorial and made another appointment to see the surgeon. Ed filled out new admittance forms and made hotel arrangements for me. Believing surgery would end Ed's miserable, horrible illness, we crossed our fingers, held hands, and naively proclaimed, "Costa Rica, here we come. Italy, too!"

One week later, as we passed Yankee Stadium on our way to keep the slated appointment at Hunter Memorial, Ed was unusually quiet. Gone was his smile from seven days ago. He seemed tense and on edge. Figuring he was tired, I offered to drive. Ed snapped. He said he didn't understand why I wanted to drive. He said he wasn't dead, yet. He said that he could take care of himself and his wife just fine. He said that I should stop telling him what to do. I had never seen Ed flip out like this. I just sat there staring out the passenger window, fighting tears. Something had set Ed off, and I worried what it was.

Later, in the doctor's examination room, Ed sat on the examination table while I stood crumpled in the corner, holding his jacket, still upset at the cross words he had spoken to me on our drive into the city. The doctor walked into the room and asked Ed to remove his shirt.

Ed fingered a button on the cuff of his sleeve. "Doctor," Ed said, "I have a lump." He held out his left arm.

I was stunned. I blinked back tears.

"When did this happen?" the doctor asked.

"I found it this morning when I got out of the shower. I didn't tell Linda, because I didn't want to upset her."

"Well," I chirped. "I'm upset now."

The doctor examined Ed's arm. He listened to his chest, thumped his back with his fist, took a step back, and said the surgery would have to be postponed. Then he asked Ed to have a special test, left the room, and returned with an adhesive cuff. He asked Ed to slip his arm inside it, explaining it was meant to restrict the blood from making any more clots. He brought in a chair for me, and after I was comfortably seated, he discussed Ed's tumor. I didn't understand one word the guy said. I said, I am a visual person, doctor; could you please draw me a picture? He did. It looked like an upside-down lollipop with an X representing the tumor placed in the spot where the stick meets the candy. He assured me that he would do everything possible to help Ed, and then he told Ed he could put his shirt back on, and he left the room. A short time later, a tall man dressed in a suit and tie entered the room. The man had a full head of hair, a glowing complexion, and a jolly, robust voice. He told us he had the same cancer as Ed and had undergone the same operation Ed was going to have. He said everything Ed was going through was just a bump in the road. He said the surgery, though difficult, would prove beneficial, and he promised he would be there to offer support. He said he was in a group with this disease and assured Ed everyone would be there for him and me. Before he walked out the room, he shook Ed's hand, gave me a hug, and wished us good luck.

On the way home, Ed apologized for being so short with me. He said, I didn't mean what I said. He said, I love you very, very much. He said, you are my wife and you are number one in my life.

He said, "I don't know why I did that."

It was a windy March afternoon the day Ed and I drove to Grace Medical Center for him to receive his special test, the test that would determine whether he could have his operation. Pacing the long sterile hallway outside the X-ray department, I fingered a crystal rosary in one pocket with one hand, a Star of David hanging off a chain looped around my neck with the other, the whole time thinking we had a chance. An hour later I was still pacing the hall when a nurse appeared to tell me the test was over, and as soon as the doctor had read the X-rays, he would be out to give us the results. I walked alongside Ed's stretcher as he was wheeled to a room filled with other outpatients waiting for test results. The room was small and cramped. A row of headboards from a dozen beds lined the wall, each separated by one aluminum folding chair and a wafer-thin curtain hanging from a U-shaped rod in the ceiling. The doctor walked to Ed's side opposite me. He yanked hard on the curtain, shrouding us in a snow-white slip of no-privacy, looked straight into my eyes, and delivered the grim news. The doctor said the tumor had grown. He said that even with chemo, there was nothing he could offer Ed. He said he was very, very sorry. And like an actor who has just delivered his lines, the good doctor parted the flimsy curtain and exited the stage. A loud hush fell over the room. Every patient and every nurse and every doctor in that small crowded space on the other side of that see-through curtain heard what the doctor said. And they got quiet. When someone did speak, it was in a soft whisper. Ed and I grabbed hold of each other and choked back tears.

It is the week before Ed's death. The weather is cold and wet. Rain pelts the windows of our townhome. It stops. The sky clears. It rains. It stops. The sky clears. Then the stormy madness begins again. We sit on the sofa watching *Law & Order*. Cuddled to the sofa arm, my chin rests in one hand, and my other hand strokes Ed's head resting in my lap. His legs are stretched, his feet propped on the opposite sofa arm. He is covered neatly in his mom's hand-knitted afghan, and we pass time, resigned to his gloomy fate, simply waiting for the angel of death, the intrusive lurker at the door, wings poised, ready to pay its gloomy visit. We know it will be soon. We know it by the eerie rattle in Ed's chest and every labored breath he takes, by his swollen feet and ankles that prevent him from wearing shoes, and by the mighty liquid swelling his lungs and puffing his fingers. We know it by the indelible furrows etched in his brow, and the gnawing that inches into his flesh, lungs, stomach, spleen, and esophagus from his insides out. I don't want Ed to see me cry. I want him to leave this world with the memory of a strong, courageous, gallant, and brave-hearted woman—not the falling-apart, weary, worn-out leaking bucket I am. So I save my tears for when I am alone. These last weeks and many days, after Ed is asleep, in the still of the night, I slip out of our bedroom, tiptoe through the moon-lit hall, down a carpeted staircase, to the opposite end of our townhome to be alone. There, in the privacy of an entry hall bathroom, I sit on the toilet seat, grab hold of the sink, and let my tears out. The thought of Ed dying and leaving me alone to live my life without him by my side gushes from deep inside me, and it is more than I can bear.

I confess I had tremendous difficulty dealing with any of it, and at the end of one long, horrible, miserable Ed-dying day, fielding twenty-five telephone calls from well-meaning friends, neighbors, business associates, coworkers, and family members, all demanding an accounting of Ed's irreversible condition while I listened stoically to their well-intentioned sad commentaries on the inevitable and how much they're going to miss their beloved brother, neighbor, friend, dad, dog-walker's ex-wife's husband's milkman's best friend's lover's tennis instructor's shoemaker's friend, I trekked up the stairs and fell into bed, curling into Ed's bare chest, and sobbed my guts out. I said, I can't take any more. I said, I am frightened, scared, fed up, and please tell me what do I do after you are ... and then I stumbled. I could not say the "d word" to my beloved husband. Not out loud. The truth that my husband was going to be dead in a short while was so ugly that I needed another word to describe it. And it was at that ugly moment I realized the sad truth. Holding back all the things the doctors had shared with me, and the research I had made about Ed's cancer, had gotten to me. I was hollow as a gutted trick-or-treat pumpkin. I felt as fake as the Easter Bunny, and for the first time in my marriage, I felt I had betrayed myself and, worse, my Ed. I let everything inside me out. I was a dam burst, and my words gushed forth. I just wanted to come clean. I needed to feel like a wife again, and not some mother nurse sister aunt friend carrying Jell-O on a tray and fielding corrosive phone calls. I was a tsunami beating a path to shore, blurting all the misery that had welled up from deep inside me for months.

What is to become of me? Where will I go? What will I do? I sobbed. Please tell me, I said. I need you to tell me, I begged. For me the question was not whether I could survive, but would I? And how? Without Ed by my side to guide me, I had no idea. My thoughts made me crazy. I buried my face in Ed's naked chest and waited for Ed to console me. I desperately needed him to place his arms around me and tell me everything would be all right. In a small voice, Ed said, "I can't tell you that." He said, "I can't tell you what to do." He said, "You have to find your own way." And then everything turned ugly. Ed got testy. He said, "I don't have time for this discussion." He rolled on his side, put his back to my face, and faced the wall. For a long while I stared into a birthmark on his flesh. There was silence, a long, eerie, starchy silence. I got out of bed and retreated to the downstairs den. In a prenatal position I curled up on the sofa and cried. I cried for Ed and his cancer. I cried for feeling guilty that Ed was sick and I was helpless to help him. I cried for being selfish. I didn't want to bury my husband. I didn't want my husband to die. I regretted unburdening myself on Ed. I felt tremendous guilt about all of it. It was as if I had been swallowed by a whale. I just lay there crying.

I didn't hear Ed kneel beside me, but I felt his touch on my shoulder and his fingers gently brush my hair. He said, "I'm sorry, Linda." Then he rose from the floor and sat down beside me. Placing his arms around me, he pulled me close, and I cried harder, thinking it was for the last time. Ed said he didn't mean to hurt my feelings. He said he was scared too. He said, I don't want to die. He said, I love you very much, and you are number one.

Then Ed broke down, and he cried. He put his face on my chest, and I felt his wet tears moisten my nightshirt. We cried together. He said, I don't want to leave you, not now, not ever. I said I was sorry too. I said it's okay to cry and to let the tears out. Then I told Ed about a writing retreat I had attended in Taos in 2001. I said everybody cries on a writing retreat. I said on a writing retreat a writer learns to write from the heart. I explained writing practice—a topic is given, I said, a timer is set, and a writer simply writes, and when the bell goes off, the signal that time is up, everybody puts down their pen and waits a turn to read what it is they just wrote. I said everybody cries reading their work out loud. I said, "If you were in Taos, and you wrote what it is you just said and read it out loud, everybody would cry with you. Then they'd hug you. You'd feel normal, whatever normal is, and you'd learn you're not alone."

Ed stopped crying. I did too. I lifted my face from the crook of his shoulder and looked into his wet eyes. The rain had stopped, and in the slip of moonlight peeking through the uncurtained window, I saw a part in his tender lips, and his radiant smile.

As the days leading up to Ed's death pass, the dying process intensifies. Each day grows longer and more horrid than the day before. I am out of words to describe it. Cancer is a hideous disease, and, I have learned, one does not light up like a neon sign upon its arrival. No bells ring, no alarms sound to usher it in, and in Ed's case, it ran like a submarine, deep, silent, and deadly. By the time the swelling appeared on his neck, the striking clue the killer was here that dark day in November 2003, it was already too late for Ed. Prolonging Ed's life was like rearranging deck chairs on board the *Titanic*. In my book, it was cruel, unnatural torture, and inhumane punishment. When the end finally came, I regretted deeply having supported his decision to have the chemo treatments. I had lived the horror observing his pain, and eventual demise, and it gave me true pause on the practice of euthanasia. I couldn't help Ed live, but at one point I realized I sure as hell could help him die, and with dignity. The days inch forward, we remind each other that soon it will be our wedding anniversary. I want so very much to have this anniversary with Ed, and he knows it. When I mention this, Ed says he wants to give me a present and asks, "Linda Please, tell me what can I give you?"

It was the eve of the eve of Ed's death, the eve of the eve of our sixteenth wedding anniversary, and it was the middle of the night. Ed had planned to take me out to dinner as celebration if he made it through the night. The weather was cold, and an endless rain poured out of the sky, melting winter snow, flooding roads, and swamping the backyard. I lie in bed, Ed at my side, the howling wind rattling the windows, pelting the shingled roof, and pinging the aluminum gutters. Distant thunder rocked the heavens while Ed, sedated by morphine, rested comfortably. Exhausted from racing the clock to keep him that way, I rested at his side atop the covers when the morphine dripping through a tube from the locked box hanging off a pole leading to his port stopped pumping. No amount of pressing the reset button on the box or the hand-held device made it work. I traced the plastic tube from pole to port, searching for the problem. I couldn't get the morphine pump to give a shot of painkiller no matter how hard, or how often, I pressed the button. Ed's pain heightened and he was crying. He needed pain medicine. He needed morphine. And he needed it now. It was two o'clock a.m. The louder Ed screamed, the more feverishly I worked to make the pump work. I never felt so impotent. Cancer pain is the worst pain on this earth. In my mind's eye, I see shark teeth racing at lightning speed, pulverizing flesh, liver, spleen, bone, and traveling ferociously to the heart and brain. Hate it. As ridiculous as it may sound, if cancer were a person, I'd shoot it dead, douse the remains in gasoline, strike a match, and set it on fire. Then I'd seal the ashes in a leaded box and dump it into the deepest sea. Try as I might, I could not get the pump to work. Every attempt failed. I gave up finally and called hospice. The answering service said my nurse, Karen Doty, was away for the weekend. This meant they would send another hospice nurse. It would take time to contact a nurse, time for that nurse to get out of her warm bed, and time for her to make the drive in the cold, dark night to where Ed lay dying.

When it is your loved one lying in pain, time crawls, and each second is an eternity. By the time the knock on the door announcing the nurse's arrival came, Ed's condition had deteriorated, along with my fragile mental state. I stared out the bedroom window, into the dark night, at trees bending in the howling wind, and I begged out loud to any god above to give an ear and please make the fucking pump work. There was a crack of lightning, a blast of thunder, and in the mirrored window, I caught a glimpse of my weary reflection—a pathetic woman with a splotch of spaghetti sauce as big as a frying pan running down the front of her shirt. My hair was greasy and matted and stuck to my head. Mascara globs oozed down my cheeks.

Two mornings past, I had left Ed's side. I was hungry. I needed a break. In a frenzy I had rushed out of our bedroom, down the stairs, and into the kitchen for something to eat. Swinging the refrigerator door open, I'd grabbed a plastic container filled with cold spaghetti and hastily removed the plastic lid. The whole thing slipped from my fingers, exploded into the front of my shirt, then crashed to the floor. Scooping up the stringy mess with my bare hands, I shoved a fistful into my mouth, wiped the floor with a paper towel, and dumped the rest into the sink, rinsing my hands in clear tap water and using the front of my shirt to wipe them dry, the entire time thinking that any moment my husband would be dead and I must be at his side. I kept thinking about Ed's promise and him saying, "Linda Please, don't worry; we'll be together for our anniversary."

Now, in the glimmer of light streaking the blackened sky, and my reflection blinking back at me, I could see the clothes I had dressed in five days earlier and realized it was just as many days since I'd showered, washed my face, brushed my teeth, and combed my hair. I was Cujo, trapped in a Stephen King novel. And I wasn't leaving my post.

The hospice nurse couldn't get the pump to work either. For whatever reason, the thing wouldn't budge. She gave Ed a dose of Ativan, hoping to temporarily relieve his pain while she dialed the manufacturer on her cell phone to ask for help. With rain, wind, lightning, and Ed screaming, I stood at his bedside hugging myself, wishing this night to end sooner than later. When the hospice nurse got through to the answering service, she was given an emergency number. She dialed it. It was after hours, and the emergency number played a recorded message. The hospice nurse pressed the speaker button, and I heard every word. "Sorry," it said. "Call back tomorrow. There's nobody here."

Sorry? Tomorrow?

Remembering the jug of liquid morphine a doctor at Hunter Memorial had prescribed, I rushed to the bathroom, flung open the cabinet, and grabbed the hefty bottle the size and color of a half-gallon jug of milk. I remember thinking at the time I filled the prescription, *Who uses this much morphine? And what kind of pain does a person gotta have to need this much?* It didn't matter. In a last-ditch effort, I uncapped the bottle, rushed to Ed's side, and placed it to his lips. Holding his mouth open with one hand and the opened bottle with the other, I poured it down his throat until the purple liquid spilled over his lips, ran down his chin to his neck and chest, and oozed through my fingers, soaking my hands to my wrists. When I had finished, I used my shirt to wipe my hands and Ed's face, adding another splotch, this one purple, to the front of my filthy shirt. In a short time, Ed closed his eyes and fell fast asleep. The hospice nurse stood beside me, stethoscope hanging around her neck. I put my ear to Ed's chest and listened to the thump-thump sound beating hard. I waited as the nurse checked his vitals, then watched as she put on her coat and left. I locked the door behind her and returned to Ed's side, one hand resting on his rising and falling chest, the other hand clasping the open bottle of morphine. If Ed awakened again in pain, I didn't give a fuck the pump didn't work. I was ready.

It was the next morning. It stopped raining, but the wind was blowing hard, and the outside temperature was very cold. In the warm sunlight streaming through the window, my shirt looked kind of pretty. I was a wild woman, and I dressed the part. It wasn't yet nine o'clock when the doorbell rang. I left Ed's side to answer it. It was the hospice nurse from last night, and accompanying her was a giant woman with a butch haircut. The woman was dressed in jeans. She wore a wide leather belt with a ring of keys hanging from it, and a leather jacket with a turned-up fur collar framing her thick neck. I thought the woman was a man until I noticed the outline of a bra through the front of her man-tailored shirt after she had removed her jacket. This was someone I had never seen before, and as soon as I opened the door, the bulky person pushed me aside and marched up the stairs to the bedroom, hollering along the way, "You can't give this man morphine. You are not authorized." Then she said, "I will call the police on you and have you arrested." Then she grabbed Ed by his shoulders and shook him. Hard. Ed let out a scream. An awful, desperate cry. It rocked me to my core, and in my mind's eye I saw a monster beating my dying husband, and I lost it.

I said, "Who are you? And what are you doing in my house?"

She said, "You can't keep me out of here!"

The weather outside changed again, and it started to rain hard. It sounded like pebbles pelting the roof. I raced to the telephone and called my personal physician. I needed help, and I needed it now! I knew Doctor D would be there for Ed. And for me. Doctor D knew Ed, and he knew about Ed's cancer. He had known me from the time I was a little girl. He knew my mom and dad and my brother. When he came to the telephone, I told him about the morphine drip not working during the night and what I had done to ease my husband's pain. I said, there is a nurse here from hospice; she says I will be arrested. I said, Ed needs his morphine dose increased. I said, he is in terrible pain. Please, I said to my doctor, please help my husband. I said, this hospice nurse refuses to help.

My doctor instructed me to give the phone to the nurse. I did. The doctor's voice crackled through the air, and I heard every word. My doctor ordered the woman to increase the morphine from two to five milligrams. He ordered her to release the dose every fifteen minutes, not every thirty minutes. The wind whistled through the trees in the backyard. The nurse argued. "You can't do that," she said.

As rain pounded the house, the good doctor's words steamrolled over hers. "You are not the doctor here," he said. "Do as you are told, or I will get someone who will."

The woman grew silent. She put down the phone, reached to her belt, unclipped her ring of keys, and clicked one into the precious slot on the morphine box. She turned the tumblers, shut the box, locked it, turned on her heels, and, like the Wicked Witch of the East, flew out the room, down the stairs, and out the door, slamming it hard behind her.

Sedated and pain-free, Ed spent the remainder of the day with me on the floor, our backs resting against the side of our queen-sized bed, bare feet touching a closed closet door, holding hands, recalling vacations, business trips, and grand parties—St. Maarten, the Museum of History in Hong Kong, his niece's elegant wedding in a posh hotel in Manhattan, the bar mitzvah of a best friend's son, and the surprise fiftieth birthday party I threw for him at the White Plains Hotel after we got married. We pretended we had tomorrow and the day after that, and we planned the places we would visit and things we would

do after we got there. Ed kept asking, what day is it? I said, it's April 30. I said, soon it will be May 1; looks like we're going to make it to number sixteen. We're together to the—. And then I stopped. Ed said, I'm sorry I can't take you to dinner. I said, It's okay. Then I began words from our wedding vows:
>Do not walk ahead of me. I may not follow.

Ed jumped in. *Do not walk behind me. I may not lead.*

Together, we said, *Just walk beside me and be my friend.*

We sat quiet, holding hands, heads resting on each other's shoulder, recalling one rainy Saturday morning on the first of May, walking First Avenue to the nondenominational chapel at 77 United Nations Plaza.

The day wore on, the sun lowered in the sky, and through the uncurtained window we watched it set.

The following day, in between carrying Ed on my back to the bathroom and returning him to the padded floor, because he was just too darn heavy to lift back in bed, we held hands and continued with stories from our past. Remember the day we moved into Rye Brook? I said. Yeah, Ed said. I remember our neighbor mistaking you for the cleaning woman. I laughed, heartily. Ed frowned. The end was here.

Outside the wind was blowing hard, and rain poured from the sky in torrents. It was after 11:30 at night. All day Ed had kept asking what day it was. I kept telling him the thirtieth of April. I began thinking that Ed, ever my faithful husband, was holding on to life for me, desperate to grant me one last wish—a gift of love. Finally, I said, it's May 1. It wasn't. Not yet. But Ed was suffering so much I began thinking, *In the big picture, what does it matter what day it is?* I said, happy anniversary, Ed. Ed said, happy anniversary, Linda. I smiled.

Ed said, "I pay the bills on the first of the month."

"I know."

"I mail them on the fifth or the sixth."

"I know."

"I have to leave now."

"I know."

"Leave with me."

"I can't. But it's okay if you leave. It's okay if you leave me. I give you permission. You're not a bad husband if you leave, Ed. You're a good husband. I love you. Forever."

"I love you too."

"I'm sorry." I started to cry. "I'm so, so sorry."

"It's not your fault."

"Don't worry 'bout me." I held his hand. "I'll be all right," I said. "I promise. I'll be your wife forever. I'll never get married again. I promise."

Ed smiled. "I will always be here for you. Always remember that."

I nodded. I held him close.

"I'll write your story," I said. I meant it. "I promise I will let the whole world know what you went through."

"Somebody should."

"Find a little house." I pressed my cheek to his. "A place with a yard for a dog and a cat. Make a little garden. Put the water on for tea. Pour me a cup and wait for me."

"I will. I promise."

"I love you."

"I love you too."

Our hands clasped. Our lips met. And we kissed our last kiss.

The rain stopped raining, the wind stopped blowing, and the clock struck twelve. And, just like that, Ed's heart stopped beating. It was May 1, 2004, our sixteenth wedding anniversary.

We made it.

For a long time I just sat there holding my dead husband in my arms, kissing him gently. Then I closed his eyes. His death wasn't ugly, as I had feared it would be. It was as if he simply left the room; as if a light switched off and his eyes went vacant. I placed my ear to Ed's chest. I pressed hard.

Nothing.

I filled a basin with warm water and placed a bar of Ivory soap in it. I dipped a thirsty washcloth and squeezed it tight. Ed lay on the floor. I knelt at his side. In life Ed had treated his body like a temple. He fussed over his clothes, polishing his shoes every night before placing them in his closet. In the course of his sickness, I noticed him sniff his underarm for body odor. That was in the early days of his sickness, when he couldn't get out of bed to shower. I knew Ed wouldn't want a stranger bathing him, so I did for him what I knew he would have done for me. I lathered his face with shaving cream, took his razor, and shaved him. I combed his hair and was amazed how fast it had grown without the chemo. Lying there on the floor, clean and peaceful, he reminded me of our wedding day sixteen years ago to the day, and the angel I had married. Ed's face was radiant.

After I bathed Ed, I kissed his body. I started at his forehead, inching to his toes. I kissed his eyes, nose, cheeks, chin, neck, left shoulder, right shoulder, left arm, right arm, chest, stomach, navel, penis, thighs, knees, calves, ankles, toes, and soles of his feet.

"Thank you," I said, "for being my husband, my lover, my knight in shining armor, my loyal best friend. And most of all, thank you for loving me back."

I couldn't help but feel Ed's presence hovering over me.

Then I covered him in a crisp white sheet. The one I stole from the hospital.

For a long time I sat at Ed's side, embracing his warm presence and saying a prayer to my dead dad to please take good care of Ed.

- 10 -

BEGINNINGS

There will be a time when all of the pieces will fit together and we will understand the reason for the pain.

Unknown

It is Monday, May 3, 2004. Wearing dark glasses, dressed in black suit, stockings, and heels, my hair covered in a black scarf, I stand numbly over a hole in the earth, and stare at a steely casket covered in yellow roses and baby's breath; a golden-haloed teddy bear the color of snow touches the center. My beloved husband is dead. My son's girlfriend Colleen, clasps my hand. She rubs my back. A yellow rose petal flutters in the breeze, while memories of a hundred days light the landscape of my brain and come to life in faded, clouded visions. As the cantor prays, I try to make sense of my broken world.

יִתְגַּדַּל וְיִתְקַדַּשׁ שְׁמֵהּ רַבָּא (אָמֵן)

Yit'gadal v'yit'kadash sh'mei raba
Amein.
May His great Name grow exalted and sanctified
Amen.

בְּעָלְמָא דִּי בְרָא כִרְעוּתֵהּ
b'al'ma di v'ra khir'utei
in the world that He created as He willed.

וְיַמְלִיךְ מַלְכוּתֵהּ בְּחַיֵּיכוֹן וּבְיוֹמֵיכוֹן
v'yam'likh mal'khutei b'chayeikhon uv'yomeikhon
May He give reign to His kingship in your lifetimes and in your days,

וּבְחַיֵּי דְכָל בֵּית יִשְׂרָאֵל
uv'chayei d'khol beit yis'ra'eil
and in the lifetimes of the entire Family of Israel,

בַּעֲגָלָא וּבִזְמַן קָרִיב וְאִמְרוּ
ba'agala uvizman kariv v'im'ru:
swiftly and soon. Now say:

אָמֵן: יְהֵא שְׁמֵהּ רַבָּא מְבָרַךְ לְעָלַם וּלְעָלְמֵי עָלְמַיָּא
Amein. Y'hei sh'mei raba m'varakh l'alam ul'al'mei al'maya
Amen. May His great Name be blessed forever and ever.

It is Christmas Eve, 2003. We are in Dr. O's office. Ed sits on an examination table. He isn't wearing a shirt. The stout man with deep-set eyes and dark hair thumps Ed's chest. He places a stethoscope to his ears. He sets the flat edge of the listening device against Ed's bare back. Ed winces at the chill of the cold metal pressing against his skin.

"Dr. O," *I say.*

The doctor removes the stethoscope from one ear.

"The doctors at Grace Medical are testing Ed for cancer," *I say.* "They think my husband has cancer."

Ed shoots a tired look at me. His message is clear. He wants me to be quiet. He doesn't want me to question his doctor's diagnosis of asthma.

Dr. O says, "There's no cancer here."

He continues to thump Ed's back, his chest. He touches the mysterious swelling on Ed's throat. Ed winces.

"I don't know what's wrong with those guys at Grace Medical," Dr. O says. "This is a healthy man. There's no cancer here. Pay no attention to them." When I look at Ed, I see his eyes. I look into his face. I start to cry.

יִתְבָּרַךְ וְיִשְׁתַּבַּח וְיִתְפָּאַר וְיִתְרוֹמַם וְיִתְנַשֵּׂא

Yit'barakh v'yish'tabach v'yit'pa'ar v'yit'romam v'yit'nasei
Blessed, praised, glorified, exalted, extolled,

וְיִתְהַדָּר וְיִתְעַלֶּה וְיִתְהַלָּל שְׁמֵהּ דְּקֻדְשָׁא

v'yit'hadar v'yit'aleh v'yit'halal sh'mei d'kud'sha
mighty, upraised, and lauded be the Name of the Holy One,

Dr. O hands Ed his shirt. He says, "She loves you, you know. She's worried about you. She's concerned."

Dr. O removes a prescription pad from his shirt pocket. He scribbles something, then hands me the slip of paper. "Here," he says. "This is my home number. Call me. I'm here for you." Then Dr. O tells us to go home. He says, "Enjoy your holiday."

בְּרִיךְ הוּא

B'rikh hu.
Blessed is He

לְעֵלָּא מִן כָּל בִּרְכָתָא וְשִׁירָתָא

l'eila min kol bir'khata v'shirata,
beyond any blessing and song,

תֻּשְׁבְּחָתָא וְנֶחֱמָתָא דַּאֲמִירָן בְּעָלְמָא וְאִמְרוּ

toosh'b'chatah v'nechematah, da'ameeran b'al'mah, v'eemru:
praise and consolation that are uttered in the world. Now say:

It is a cold February afternoon. The ground is a blanket of white. Ed and I have driven to Mount Calvary Cemetery for an appointment to pick out our cemetery plot. In keeping with Jewish tradition, Ed requests a side-by-side plot. I have offered for Ed to be buried in the Jewish cemetery with his parents in New Haven, Connecticut. Ed will have none of it. The Jewish cemetery will not take me. I am a baptized Catholic. There is a nonsectarian cemetery not far from our home. I suggest that cemetery. Ed dislikes that idea. Instead, he chooses Mt. Calvary, the Catholic cemetery where my parents, Frank and Grace Della Donna; grandparents Gasparo and Josephine Siciliano; baby niece, Jennifer Sporkmann; and Siciliano aunts, uncles, and cousins are buried. Over the years, Ed has accompanied me on visits to my parents' grave, placing a rock on their headstone, the Jewish custom, a sign that a loved one has paid a visit. He knows I will visit there. When I call the cemetery caretaker to make the appointment, a woman answers the phone and says, "Oh, yes, we take Jews here, so long as one of the married partners is a Catholic. We have quite a few Jews here," she says.

אָמֵן

Amein
Amen.

"Can my husband have a Star of David on the headstone?" I ask.
The woman assures me Ed can, so long as it is a tiny star. "We cannot offend the other Catholics," she says.

יְהֵא שְׁלָמָא רַבָּא מִן שְׁמַיָּא

Y'hei sh'lama raba min sh'maya
May there be abundant peace from Heaven

The sky is gun metal gray. Ed doesn't walk with me. He just stands at the crest of the road a short distance away, alongside the rugged caretaker, and stares blankly in my direction. His hands are jammed inside his jacket pockets, fine silken threads of hair whisk out of his Mets' baseball cap and whip his puffed, pale face as I sink through the crusted snow, pacing from one plot to the next, inspecting each one as if I am sizing up a lot to build a house on. Everywhere is snow and the air is frigid. One lone buffalo cloud drifts ominously above our heads. My back to Ed and facing the snowy hill below, I see the road tucked into the rocky horizon. Pressed into the snowy landscape is the outline of a frozen pond, a giant stone altar resting against a life sized Christ figure hanging off a giant cross, and rows of snow-covered monuments punctuating the linen-white vision. Trying to make light of the distasteful task, I point and blurt, "Look! This one has a view."

When I turn to face Ed, he is wiping his eyes.

וְחַיִּים עָלֵינוּ וְעַל כָּל יִשְׂרָאֵל וְאִמְרוּ

v'chayim aleinu v'al kol yis'ra'eil v'im'ru
and life upon us and upon all Israel. Now say:

I return to Ed's side, and the rugged cemetery man asks Ed if he has any preference. Ed says the choice isn't up to me. He says, it is up to my wife. Ed says, Linda must make this decision.

אָמֵן

Amein
Amen.

עֹשֶׂה שָׁלוֹם בִּמְרוֹמָיו הוּא יַעֲשֶׂה שָׁלוֹם

Oseh shalom bim'romav hu ya'aseh shalom
He Who makes peace in His heights, may He make peace,

עָלֵינוּ וְעַל כָּל יִשְׂרָאֵל וְאִמְרוּ

aleinu v'al kol Yis'ra'eil v'im'ru
upon us and upon all Israel. Now say:

אָמֵן

Amein
Amen.

The cantor has finished praying, and my clouded Ed image standing in the distance peering back at me has faded. Colleen takes my hand and leads me to the waiting limousine.

"Is it over?"

"Yes."

Part II

THE FIRST THREE YEARS

- 11 -
GRATITUDE

Mourning the death of a loved one is like licking
a block of dry ice. It hurts to let go.

When I was first married to Ed, I tried to imagine what my life would be like if he were dead. Not the morbid sickness, sadness, or misery that goes with watching a soul mate die, but the way I would conduct myself if he were gone. I'd stand at the kitchen sink, elbow-deep in suds, imagining I'd be strong as Jackie O, as courageous as Coretta Scott King, and as charitable as Eleanor Roosevelt. *No problem*, I thought. *No problem*.

After a time I'd forget about my trio of widows and begin complaining about my boring nine-to-five job, while Ed, just in from a hard day at the office, a blanket of unopened bills spread out on the table before him, sat quietly and listened. Toweling my hands, I'd watch as he'd rip open each envelope, scan the contents, pocket household bills for payment later, crumple and toss junk mail in the trash, the entire time nodding and smiling. If Ed had had a bad day, if the electric bill was too high, if the water pump in his Camry had exploded on the Triboro Bridge on his way to the office that morning, or if the airplane he had flown in the day before had stuttered and sputtered in air turbulence thirty thousand feet in the sky, I had no clue. He was that good.

Nothing lasts forever. Not summer vacations, careers, or childhood. Not even my precious marriage. Watching Ed get sick and die was difficult. And saying good-bye to a man who loved life and was so darn good at living it, well, it takes time for the brain to wrap itself around the ugly thought that he is never coming back. Let the world know, I didn't have a good marriage—I had a *great* marriage. And I knew it. I always knew it. Like two chips in a cookie, we were rolling along, when *bam*! My husband gets a cancer and dies, leaving me a widow.

What was I thinking? *No problem*? Ha! After Ed died I was lifeless as a windsock after a storm. I was rocked to my core. I didn't eat. I didn't sleep. I couldn't concentrate. I was bereft.

As time wore on I became aware of grief triggers. They lurked everywhere, and always when I least expected, they reared their ugly heads, making me an out-of-control puddle. One afternoon while pushing a grocery cart down the cereal aisle in my local supermarket, I burst into tears. One look at a colorful trademarked toucan perched on front of a Kellogg's cereal box, Ed's favorite breakfast treat, the message that my Ed was dead and was never coming back shot my brain. Gasping for breath, I abandoned my cartful of groceries, rushing for the exit, the entire time thinking, *I don't want to live, not without Ed by my side. It's just too dang painful!*

On top of that, I suffered tremendous guilt. My husband was dead, and all I could think was, *It's all my fault!* I told myself I should have known he was sick. I was his wife. I said, *Self, if you hadn't spent so much time scribbling in spiral-bound notebooks, you might have noticed your husband had a cancer.* It wasn't until Ed's sister, Judy, had collapsed on Vail Mountain on a ski vacation less than a year and a half later that I changed my thinking. Tests revealed Judy had an inoperable tumor, and within three months she was dead. Judy was a Vassar graduate, and her husband, Jim, graduated Yale medical. It hit me that if doctor Jim didn't know his beloved wife was sick with a cancer, how could writer

Linda know her beloved husband was sick with the same dread disease? Though deeply saddened by Judy's death, for the first time since Ed's death I breathed a sigh of joyous relief, realizing it wasn't my fault my husband was dead. It was at that moment I knew I was one baby step forward in processing my grief, but I still had a long way to go. For close to two years, I tried managing my grief alone, and with no good results. I had dropped eighteen pounds, and when I looked in the mirror at my gaunt reflection, I had to admit that I needed help. I reached out to a priest, a truly kindhearted man at White Plains Episcopalian Church, and sincerely interested in helping me. Together we lit a candle, knelt before a statue of the Virgin Mary, and prayed a Hail Mary. It was nice to pray for the soul of a Jewish man in a Christian setting, but I didn't feel better.

I met with a Buddhist monk at a converted storefront temple on Broadway in Dobbs Ferry. While a frail man draped in pumpkin orange burned incense and said prayers for Ed's reincarnation, I sat silent, barefoot, and numb. The monk said I did a good thing helping Ed into his next life, and that I should feel proud, but the thought of Ed living a good life someplace else without me by his side made me crazy.

I made an appointment with a psychiatrist, where I stared at my feet while pouring my heart out, telling how Ed had suffered and died and that I missed him very much. When I looked to see why the strange man with two diplomas hanging on the wall over his desk hadn't responded, I saw he was gazing out an open window. He hadn't listened to one word I had said. But he wrote me a prescription for Lexapro and showed me to the door. After tossing the prescription in the trash, I met with a psychologist. Three framed diplomas hung over her desk. When she looked out the window, I got up and showed myself to the door.

I met with a rabbi. I liked the rabbi. He told jokes. I didn't laugh.

I met with my family doctor, and after I had described what it was I was going through, he advised me to keep searching. He said not to be discouraged, that it takes time to find the right therapist when working through grief. He said his wife was a counselor, and suggested I see her. I did. When she talked, this time I stared out the window.

I joined a bereavement group in White Plains. I hated it.

I attended a different bereavement group. This one was at Westchester Jewish on Central Avenue, around the corner from my townhome. I hated that one also, but the therapist who ran it made a favorable impression on me. She was a widow. She smiled. She laughed. She made me laugh. She gave me hope, and at the end of the session, I asked privately if we could meet one-on-one. She said she didn't do one-on-one counseling, but that she could refer me to someone who did. I took a chance and jotted down the name, Karen Dreher, along with a telephone number. The following day I called the number and made an appointment.

Karen is a counselor who specializes in grief, and, I learned, there is a difference. Immediately, Karen and I connected. I have no idea why. But thanks to Karen and her patience and understanding, and a lot of hard work on my part, I made it through much misery and my grief.

May 1, 2007, marked the third anniversary of Ed's death. Winter was done. Snow had fallen. Snow had melted. Spring had sprung. In my mind's ear, I heard Ed's voice, *Linda Please, I can't stand it if you're unhappy.* When I looked out my bedroom window, I saw my world had changed. The sun shone brightly; a crimson-breasted robin strutted the driveway, a wiggly earthworm the color of chocolate dangling from his golden beak. Emerald leaves sprouted from honey daffodils edging the garden path. I dashed outside and wrapped my arms around a flowering plum in the front yard. Before I knew it, I was back inside, finger-hugging my pen, and writing my heart out. Across the top line of the page, I scribbled words: *Mourning Joy*. I was healing, and I was writing my book. I wasn't sure what direction my pen was headed, but I didn't care. I just let my words rip across the page, and when I was finished writing, I realized I was in control of my tears. I told myself, *Self, if you can manage your tears, you can do anything, including fulfilling your promise to Ed.*

The next morning, I jumped out of bed and announced to the world that I was sick and tired of feeling sick and tired. I said it to my small dog, Izzy; I said it to my pillow and bathroom mirror. I strutted downstairs and said it to the kitchen sink and living room fireplace. I poked my head out my office window and said it to the flowering plum, the one I had hugged the day before. I leashed Izzy, slid the dining room slider open, and stepped outside into glorious sunshine. I inhaled, exhaled, and said it to the large looming rock. I stepped off the deck, and while Izzy lifted his leg and peed on a lilac bush, my eyes searched the heavens in a turquoise sky, and I screamed, "Ed!"

Yes, I believe.

I said, Ed, I just can't take being alone anymore. I said, I understand that the dead gotta do whatever it is the dead gotta do. But so do the living. I said, I realize my tears and carrying on the way I have been doing all this time are holding us both back from moving forward. I said, I give you permission to move forward, and I ask permission from you to do the same. I said, I need to find someone to love. I said, I hope you don't mind. I said, Please understand. I said, I will always love you. I said, I believe we will meet again, and I promise I will never forget you. Then I said, if ever I need you, not to worry, I promise, I will call on you. Then I said, you should go. I said, I don't want you hanging around anymore worrying about me. I said, I am here and you are somewhere else, and my living life like a river isn't good for either one of us.

That's when this monarch butterfly appeared. Swear to God.

That butterfly fluttered to the lilac bush Izzy had just peed on. It hovered in my face, and then it alighted on the grass at my feet. I knelt and touched it. I was so close to it, and it sat so still. Gently, I cupped my two hands over that butterfly, and the amazing thing was, it let me. That butterfly didn't move. Carefully, I slipped one hand under it and felt its whisker feet tiptoe in the palm of my hand. I felt its wafer wings brush my fingers. I parted two of them, and I saw button eyes the color of coal peek back at me. I got scared. I had never held a butterfly before. I had all I could do to keep from throwing my hands in the air and letting it go. But I didn't. I just cupped my fingers tight. I thought maybe this butterfly was Ed, and maybe he was trying to send me a message. I wanted to rush into the house and stick that butterfly in an empty glass mayonnaise jar. I didn't want to ever let that butterfly go. Then it hit me. Butterflies can't live in glass jars, and I wanted my butterfly, my Edward, to live! I couldn't bear the thought of watching that butterfly die. I opened my hands to set that butterfly free, but that butterfly didn't move. His coal-colored eyes just glistened back at me. They reminded me of fat black diamonds. It was eerie. It was strange. I looked around to see if anyone was watching. I wanted a witness. There was no one. There was just this butterfly sitting in the palms of my open hands moving its wings ever so slowly. I cried, and I began to talk to the butterfly, whispering that butterflies are free. I said it over and over. Again. Again. I said, it's okay if you fly away. I said, I'll be okay. I said, I promise. Then I held my hands high above my head. That butterfly still didn't fly. I figured it must be sick or something, and it was as if time stood still. Tiny whiskers, yellow wings, and black eyes glistening in sunlight gazing back at me.

I shook my hands. Hard harder hardest. I didn't want to hold that butterfly anymore. It didn't feel right. Its eyes grew bigger and blacker, and it began to lose its splendor. Suddenly, that butterfly burst into flight. It fluttered about my shoulders. It rose to my eyes and head. It fluttered up and down, and then it fluttered high. I watched as it fluttered to the sky, over the oak trees, into the turquoise horizon, fading into a distant milky cloud. For a moment I just stood there, looking up at the fading, bouncing dot. When I didn't see it anymore, I dried my eyes, gathered Izzy, and returned to my townhome. In the privacy of the upstairs bedroom, the one I had shared with Ed when he was alive, the place he died, I stood before my dresser, looked at my reflection in the mirror, and removed the band of gold Ed had slipped on my finger nineteen years before. My Ed was dead. My butterfly was gone. I didn't feel sad. I was filled with joy, and I was grateful!

Part III

MY LIFE TODAY

- 12 -

MOURNING JOY

And sometime when I wasn't looking, I got a new life.

At the writing of this book, it is six years, seven months, and nine days that Ed is dead and buried. Hartsdale is gone. Along with the guard and gatehouse, Olympic-sized swimming pool, double tennis courts, clubhouse with river rock fireplace and private exercise room. Three years after burying Ed, I made the decision to sell the home I shared with him the last six years of his life and move forward with the rest of mine. It was time. It was my time.

Shedding tears of what I lovingly refer to as mourning joy, I kissed good-bye the place where Ed died, bade fond farewell to the large, looming rock planted in wooded view out a bedroom window, bade adieu to the place that had anchored me to my haunting past, and set out for love and adventure in my new world, taking with me life's valuable lesson that when you lose a spouse, life goes on.

Save for Ed's aunt Rose's antique desk, his lime green bathrobe, two Cross pens, three wool sweaters, five wristwatches, one gold wedding band, and an old king-sized orange bed sheet—you know the one—what didn't get passed on to family, sold in a tag sale, or donated to Goodwill, Big Brothers Big Sisters, or the Salvation Army, got kicked to the curb. I would like to say that it bothered me watching passersby in speeding cars screech to a halt and pick through the bricks and bones of my former life, but truth is, it did not. Quite the contrary. Witnessing anonymous strangers rummage through my once-treasured items made me recall the solid sacrifices Ed and I had made to possess them, and it left me wanting less of what I had, and wishing more for what I didn't. Even now, as I sit and type these words, I can't help but think I got the better of the bargain seeing all those things get carted away and it not costing me one thin dime to have it done. Ed would have liked that.

Today, home is a cozy one-bedroom apartment in the hub of Westchester County. With money from the sale of Hartsdale, I purchased a new place, had it gutted, renovated, and decorated to my specifications. Every square inch of all 740 square feet, like my life, is utilized to the fullest. Using the elegant hotel suite Ed and I stayed in each January when attending the Annual Toy Fair in Hong Kong at the Royal Garden Hotel in Kowloon and a yacht I crewed for more than two years as guides, I created a living space fit for one contented widow living life joyously—*Me*.

Located twenty-three miles north from where the World Trade Center used to be, my humble, crimson-bricked, circa-1950 abode with concrete entry and wrought iron banisters with parking lot view, is home sweet home now. It is where a teapot whistles, guarded secrets of my present roam free, and I get a little writing done. The best part is, at the end of any given day, when I put my key in the door, I am reminded with every twist and turn in the lock of the good person I have become and the better person I am yet to be.

On frosty winter nights when the wind howls and bends the white birch outside my window, I bundle in Ed's bathrobe, curl before the TV, and sip tea out of a gray-and-pink ceramic mug, admiring its Emerson quotation and remembering. Most days, Ed's gold wedding ring, the one I slipped on his finger the day of our marriage, and removed on the same date sixteen years later, adorns the pointer finger on my right hand. Often I write with one of Ed's Cross pens; it acts as a reminder each time I make a scribble in a spiral notebook that Ed is beside me content in the knowledge that his wife is doing okay. From time to time, I wear one of Ed's wristwatches. Or one of his woolen sweaters and inhale his blessed scent. No longer do I burst into tears at their sight, aroma, or touch, for they trace the thread of golden memories when my life was richer than a king's ransom and endlessly bright. And, as I have discovered, continues to be, so long as I let it.

- 13 -

HOPE

The end of the story is never the end of the story.

--Jillian Sullivan

On January 31, 2010, I sat at my desk in my apartment and gazed into a blank computer screen. Out my window, beyond a hedge-trimmed macadam path, beyond a parking lot and busy street, snow fluttered in a clouded sky. The only sounds in the air were those of the breath in my nose, a neighbor's ringing telephone filtering through the wall, and my inner voice repeating over and over, *I did it.*

For a long time after the telephone stopped ringing, I stared blankly at a vacant green dog collar with two shiny tags dangling from its silver loop that I cradled in my hands. My book was written, and my beloved dog, Izzy, was dead.

After fourteen years and three months of Izzy's giving me unconditional love, I was faced with the ugly task of putting Ed's and my beloved dog to sleep. It was like cutting off my right arm.

As Dr. Adian at Park Animal Hospital stuck the needle in a catheter in Izzy's right paw, I held my dog close and whispered softly, *I'm sorry, I'm so, so sorry. I love you, Izzy. Go to Ed.*

When the deed was done, I unbuckled his collar, swaddled him in soft flannel, kissed his snout, caressed him one last time, and left, but not before taking one last look over my shoulder at my faithful furry friend and inhaling the sweet image of the devoted dog Ed and I had shared.

I made no promises to Izzy on his deathbed. I simply moved softly out the door and I drew on the lessons learned by saying so long to Ed, celebrating immediately, Izzy's life and the unconditional love he gave me.

The Merritt Parkway is a winding road I had traveled many times, always with Izzy at my side. This trip there was no Izzy. There was just me. And soon as my foot hit the gas pedal of my Corolla, tears gushed down my face as memories rippled.

I remembered after Ed's funeral, after every dish in the sink had been washed, dried, and put away, and after every sated mourner had departed, it was precious Izzy, curled round as a button at foot of my bed, left to tackle the mighty chore of encouraging and motivating me into believing everything would be all right.

I remembered the frosty December evening in 1995 and the barking cardboard box Ed had toted out of the Danbury Mall, the box with the furry heartbeat inside it—one scrappy happy dog.

As I scribble off into the sunset, dear reader, one thought lights my brain—it's Ed's turn to walk Izzy now, and someday we'll all meet again.

Yes, I believe.

Epilogue

A lot has happened in my life since burying Ed. In keeping an open mind and embracing change, I met many wonderful people. I made new friends. I discovered it's not about what's over the rainbow; it's more about the yellow brick road, the people we meet, and the friends we make along the way.

As with the gutting of the old apartment I moved into, and the reconstruction of it, I worked on my inner self, repairing, rebuilding, and evolving, which I continue to do on a daily basis, just like you.

I learned when you lose a spouse, it is necessary to give something back. So shortly after Ed's death, I searched my soul and scoured the earth for ways to reach out and touch someone in need.

When Hurricane Katrina struck, I raised my hand and volunteered with the American Red Cross, shipping out to Montgomery, Alabama. For three weeks I drove a truck delivering supplies and hooking up VSAT dishes at shelters south of the Mason-Dixon Line.

For a lot of Christmas seasons, I hung out on a busy street corner in Rye Brook, ringing a bell, collecting funds for the Salvation Army. This past holiday season, I rang the bell in White Plains, New York. I was awarded a wooden plaque for my work. Imagine, I raised the most amount of money in nickels, dimes, and quarters for a good cause. I have dished food to the hungry in the Episcopalian church soup kitchen, collected and distributed presents for the Port Chester Salvation Army.

In 2007, I held A Walk with Karen, honoring Karen Doty. Karen was Ed's hospice nurse, a loving woman with more than thirty years of dedicated service. Karen died suddenly, less than three years after burying Ed. I miss Karen and I will remember her with love and respect forever.

For two summers, along with faithful companion Izzy, I worked on board a yacht, cruising ports from Westport, Connecticut, to Nantucket. I learned boating and kayaking, earned my safe boating certificate, and made treasured friends at Saugatuck Harbor Yacht Club. I wasn't a member of that prestigious club, but I was treated as if I were. If it hadn't been for Ed dying, I might never have met Judy H, Kathy B, Lucia B, Sam B, Commodores B and N, Pequito, and other good members.

For three years I attended Beth Emeth Synagogue, of Larchmont, New York. I am not of the Jewish faith, but Friday evenings and Saturday mornings, for just as many years after burying Ed, I stood proudly before a Bema reciting Mourner's Kaddish. A brass plaque commemorating Ed adorns a back wall. I had it placed there. While attending services, I made friends with Rabbi K, Karen G, Spencer B, and others, who in keeping with Jewish tradition, welcomed this grieving widow with loving arms.

In 2005 I founded a website, Griefcase.net, for individuals going through the grief process, which offers interviews, tips, advice, and shared resources.

In 2010, during the renovations of my apartment and the writing of this book, I wrote on my Facebook wall that my floors were being done. I said I was going to a motel to write and would be offline a couple of days. In no time, Joyce R responded, "Linda, you are welcome here. Stay as long as you like." I hadn't seen Joyce in more than forty years. If it hadn't been for Ed dying, this rekindled friendship might never have happened.

Since Ed's death, I have written more than fifty free e-zine articles for widows, and a free e-book, *Treasury of Quotations*. My free articles can be found at Griefcase.net and ezinearticles.com. My free e-book is offered at www.griefcase.net.

Through Griefcase.net, I have interviewed hundreds of men and women who have experienced loss. Widows write me about their grief process, asking for advice and solace. Always I write back, giving reassurance that *we* are not alone.

At the writing of this book, a second book, newsletter, free e-book, confidential bereavement site, Linda's Place, and special writing retreats are in the works. I love my widow friends.

In December 2010, I returned to Mabel Dodge Luhan Lodge, Taos, for a silent writing retreat and to work on my book. During my extended stay I was invited to attend Mabel's private Christmas party. Yes, I am grateful.

In the midst of raucous renovations in my teeny-tiny apartment space, I wrote this book and fulfilled my promise to Ed, commemorating the magical date of May 1—my marriage to Ed Sclier—and the poignant date of his death.

With Ed no longer by my side to captain my journey, I handle money, balance a checkbook, pay bills, order groceries, and bake angel food cakes, and chocolate chip cookies too. I toss salads, leaving out the jumbo-sized black pitted olives, of course, and make meat ravioli.

Do I make mistakes? Yes. I make lots of mistakes. But I hold my head erect when they happen, because with each new error that I make in my new life, I discover new lessons learned and new rewards.

Most important, I conquer my fear. For I have learned it is better to pick myself up, dust myself off, and try, try, try again than to sit on my hands and watch the world go by.

If you are wondering if this widow writer dates, the answer is yes, I date. I have even kissed a fool; okay, I kissed two fools. I fell in love once; okay, I fell in love a couple of times. I grew my hair down to my waist, wear fake fingernails, and dare to polish my toenails lime green. Since losing Ed, I have learned I can laugh out loud—heartily! I can sing and dance, drive a tractor, steer a yacht, change a flat tire on a Corolla, recharge a dead battery in a Miata, snake a bathroom drain for a lost ring, make a dinner reservation for one at La Manda's Restaurant in Greenburgh, eat a slice of pizza at Michael's on North Broadway, dine at Esposito's in Valhalla, purchase a ticket out of a machine to ride a Metro North train to Grand Central, and hail a cab to see a Broadway show—alone. And enjoy it!

Do I miss Ed? You betcha! I think of Ed every day. And I will miss him till the day I die. But, as Betty Rollins says, "You don't want to be miserable all your life." I agree—heartily!

What I want you to know, dear reader, what I want you never to forget and always to remember long after this writer is dead and buried, is this: There is no right way, there is no wrong way to mourn the death of a husband. There is just your way. I can't tell you when it is a good time to get on with the rest of your life; nobody can. But you'll know it when it happens. Until that time, whenever it is you make your decision to take that flying leap, do it. Just do it. Do not be afraid to let go.

If I can do it, so can you!

Acknowledgments

I am indebted to so many for so many endless acts of loving-kindness.

First and foremost, to my brother, Richard Della Donna: You are the greatest! To my son, George Griffin, and his wife, Colleen: Thank you for my two Minion muses: grandchildren Hunter and Zoey. I love you both to the moon and back, forever! To cousins Karen, Erika, and Kerry Day: Thanks for the memories, and God bless!

To Kent Brown, the fine staff at Highlights Foundation, and most especially, Christine French Cully: Kent, thank you for believing in me and guiding me back to the blank page. Thank you for Uncle Jack's cabin, cabin #15, a place near and dear to my heart, where beginning pages for this story happened and where seven years later I discovered courage to publish it. Thank you for introducing me to enlightening teachers Jillian Sullivan and Clara Gillow Clark. Without Jillian's encouragement this book might never have been published. Jillian helped in its structure and the loving Clara was instrumental in the final version. Thank you for placing gentle, enlightened Christine in my path. Thank you, Christine, for brightening my lonely summer in Chatauqua, 2004.

To Mable Dodge Luhan Lodge, Taos, New Mexico, to Marie and delicious staff: Thank you for a lasting happy holiday memory, for warm, silent space to write, and your friendship.

To Emma Gleissman, Fatima al Mazuri, Lisa Williams, Brandon G, and Nathan at Archway Publishing. Thank you.

To others who provided friendship, support, validation, words of encouragement and/or who read different versions of this book and made helpful suggestions (in no particular order): Tom Johnson, Jillian Sullivan, Faye Levow, Donna McDine, Taryn Simpson, Neola Mace, Clara Gillow Clark, Kent Brown, Lorna Penland, 1,500 Facebook friends, members of Linda's Place, and supporters of BookOrBust.blogspot.com and Griefcase.net: Thank you.

For uninterrupted table space and freedom to work on my manuscript, hot coffee, breakfast, sandwiches, cold sodas, and iced tea, special thanks to Starbucks, Rye Ridge; Panera Bread, White Plains; Atlanta Bread, White Plains; Li'l Spot, North White Plains; Vinny's City Line Deli, North White Plains; Michael's Pizzeria, North White Plains; Carmine's Deli, Elmsford; Dunkin' Donuts, North White Plains, White Plains Public Library; Casa Rina's, Thornwood; Caffe Tazza, Taos.

To my wonderful widow friends and Facebook friends whom I have yet to meet, and my Elmsford and Sleepy Hollow friends, Robert Gaglione, Joanne Gaglione, Robert Venuti, Peggy Bauman Gallagher, and Chincoteague Ponies: Thank you. You inspire me to keep on keeping on.

Favorite places of inspiration: Green Beach, White Plains; New Milford Green, Connecticut; Oakland Beach, Rye; Chincoteague Island, Virginia; Uncle Jack's cabin, cabin #15, Mirror Lake Inn.

To Sister Mary Ancilla, RDC, my sixth-grade teacher, and Mr. Richard L. Goodwin, my tenth-grade teacher: Sister, you were first person to call me writer; Mr. G., you were second. Thank you both for planting the seed.

To Pretend Kitty: What would I do without your pretend meows reminding me to get out of bed and write?

To Izzy: Forever my muse.

I wish to remember my mother and father, Grace and Frank Della Donna: You are gone, but not forgotten. And yes, love is forever.

Finally, to Sir Galahad: You light up my life.

A Note about the Author

Linda Della Donna makes her home with a pretend kitty in White Plains, New York. A freelance writer and photographer, Della Donna is an inspirational speaker and grief coach. Some of her work has appeared in *Westchester Parent* and the *Journal News*.

Notes